You Don't Find Water on the Mountaintop

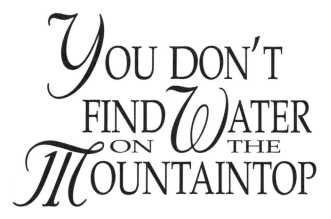

You Don't Find Water on the Mountaintop

Discovering Nourishment in Life's Valleys

Wayne Monbleau

Fleming H. Revell
A Division of Baker Book House Co
Grand Rapids, Michigan 49516

© 1996 by Wayne Monbleau

Published by Fleming H. Revell
a division of Baker Book House Company
P.O. Box 6287, Grand Rapids, MI 49516-6287

Printed in the United States of America

Library of Congress Cataloging-in-Publication Data

Monbleau, Wayne, 1952–
    You don't find water on the mountaintop : discovering nourish-
ment in life's valleys / Wayne Monbleau.
       p.   cm.
    ISBN 0-8007-5581-2 (pbk.)
    1. Suffering—Religious aspects—Christianity.   2. Hope—Religious aspects—Christianity.   3. Trust in God—Christianity.   I. Title.
BT732.7.M66   1996
248.8'6—dc20   95-38911

Contents

Introduction

Why Is This Happening to Me?

*H*ave you ever, just once, felt like striding into church and screaming at the top of your lungs, "I can't take it anymore!"? Most likely, people would look at you as if you had three heads. Why? Because we don't do things like that. We don't talk about our pain. It's not "spiritual" to do that. So, regardless of what we feel or what our circumstances may be, we steel ourselves, slap on our best Sunday-go-to-meeting smile, and pretend all is well, while inwardly we may be crying out to God.

Why is it some people are able to transcend the most terrible of circumstances while others seem to be completely overwhelmed by far lesser difficulties? Why do some seem to gain new strength from their adversities while others fall into deep bitterness against God and all of life as a result of their suffering?

These are the questions and issues I've set out to explore within these pages. This book is written for those of us (all of us, I suspect) who have suffered through, or who are suffering through, great times of darkness and despair. I don't mean the everyday petty annoyances or common difficulties we all face, but those times when all is completely dark and God seems to have taken His promises and gone on vacation. Times when you've given your all, and God, behind a thick wall of silence, seems to demand still more. As we take an honest look together at this enigmatic and mysterious side of God, my belief is that we will see even His darkness becoming light (Ps. 139:12).

Like it or not, we all suffer. Regarding His heavenly Father, Jesus stated, "He causes His sun to rise on the evil and the good, and sends rain on the righteous and the unrighteous" (Matt. 5:45). Does it ever strike you as a bit strange that so few, indeed if any, are willing to admit that life can be filled with one painful experience after another? Well, it can be, can't it? I've come to believe the sooner we accept this fact, the sooner we will begin seeing above the darkness of our immediate trials to the light of the higher-life principles being worked out within us during these dark times.

In my own reading, I've come across a mere handful of books where this apparent "dark side" of God is even hinted at. It gives me the impression that maybe we're hoping our trials will go away if we just ignore them. What's popular in Christian literature today? You know—how-to books telling us how to avoid suffering and how to have whatever we want. So, I guess this is what we want to hear. We are naturally attracted to the idea that if we quote a few Scripture passages and stand on our confession, then Shazam!—all of our problems will evaporate like morning mist as we rejoice in our victory.

Of course, ideas like this have an understandable appeal. After all, who would want to live a life of suffering? The only problem is, the people I know have very real trials that don't seem to disappear when some Scripture verse is waved over them like a magic wand.

What kind of people am I talking about? Unrepentant sinners or wishy-washy backsliders? No, I'm speaking about people who love God and have dedicated their lives to Him. Up till now, it seems our main way of dealing with this all-important issue has simply been to deny suffering or play "the blame game," projecting guilt onto the person who is dealing with trials, or blaming our own suffering on people and circumstances around us, as if the issue is whose fault it is.

Perhaps talking about pain and suffering threatens us. The truth is, many folks expend so much energy burying their own hurts that they run from anyone exposing their pain out of a fear of facing their own. So the sad situation is that we may all be hurting, but we keep up the facade, pretending we're walking in sunshine and victory.

All too often people are simply pushed aside and ignored, labeled as deficient in faith or, in extreme cases, disfellowshipped or ostracized if they dare to rip off the mask of blissful contentment and confess that their lives are falling apart. When all else fails, there's the ever popular "secret-sin-in-your-life" approach that Christians cast on fellow believers whenever they run out of explanations for the difficulties in their lives. Because most people don't know how to deal with their own pain effectively, they are left with no alternative but to silence anyone who *does* attempt to bring their own darkness out into God's light.

I think we need to wake up to reality. I'm doubtful about our ability to make meaningful progress in our spiritual lives as long as we ignore or deny our pain. Contrary to what many believe, I think our faith need not be weakened if we examine the existence of suffering in the Christian life. If we have doubts about God in our hearts, then let's get them out in the open. If we repress our secret thoughts and fears, we only fool ourselves and intensify our suffering. But by facing our doubts squarely, I believe we can begin the challenging and rewarding task of growing in the midst of our adversity. It is right here, in our pit of darkness, that we may come to terms with the purpose of suffering in our lives.

In the midst of this discussion I believe that sooner or later we will come face-to-face with the perhaps frightening but ultimately liberating truth that God is inviting each of us, in our suffering, to follow Him in becoming wounded healers.

Keep Your Eyes
on the Light

$\mathcal{I}$ had never experienced such a complete darkness and life-threatening danger like this before.

Originally, our plan was to make it a half-day hike. We were going to snowshoe a little more than a mile into New Hampshire's White Mountains National Forest. Our state's largest waterfall, Arethusa, was our destination.

Winters in northern New Hampshire are long and extremely cold. If you don't get outdoors every once in a while, you can easily develop what they call "cabin fever." In plain English, you go stir crazy. Living inside four walls from December through March can get to you if you don't watch out. It's usually pretty well into April before the snow finally subsides up here in the mountains.

We had been cooped up long enough. It was time to get outdoors. Since we had seminary classes Tuesday through Saturday, Monday was a free day. So my fellow student

Dave Smith and I called our friend John Jaworowski and talked him into joining us. As we made the forty-minute drive, we looked forward to hiking this familiar trail.

We descended into the Crawford Notch. Shaped by the movement of glaciers thousands of years ago, with mountains rising steeply on either side, the Crawford Notch is crisscrossed with a network of trails which, for those who care to make the effort, reveal the stunning beauty of God's creation. I parked my car in the lot at the entrance to the Arethusa Falls trail. We were dressed warmly, our lunches tucked away in our backpacks. I also carried a "space blanket," just in case.

The hike was strenuous and absolutely breathtaking. The saying "no pain, no gain" certainly holds true for hiking these mountain paths. On this crystal clear day, fresh fallen snow was draped over the virgin pines. Sunlight pouring through the trees reflected off the snow in a dazzling display of rainbow colors.

We finally reached our destination, the spectacular Arethusa Falls. A sheer two-hundred-foot drop over a granite cliff straight into the waiting basin below, Arethusa in the summertime would bathe you with its spray if you ventured too close. But now, in the dead of winter, the falls were frozen solid from top to bottom. A two-hundred-foot wall of ice sparkled in the sunlight. If you listened closely, you could just hear the sound of falling water behind this frozen facade.

Seated near the foot of the falls, we broke out our packed lunches. As we rested from our journey, enjoying our surroundings on this beautiful day, our spirits were refreshed. Have you ever walked so far into the woods that the only sounds you hear are the ones God created? A profound stillness overtakes you. It's almost as if you shrink while God becomes magnified many times over.

As we finished lunch, we agreed it seemed a shame to head back and bring to a close our winter wonderland experience. There was another trail. If we wanted to, instead of turning around, we could continue on up to Frankenstein Cliffs. From there it would be a hop, skip, and a jump down to the smaller Ripley Falls and then out to the road. It seemed like a great idea at the time, so we decided to "go for it."

How do you follow a trail in the deep woods with over three feet of snow on the ground? Each of these paths is color coded; that is, you can follow the path by looking for the blue markers painted on the trees. When you arrive at one tree, look for the next blue marker ahead of you and then proceed.

This is what we decided to do. But as we climbed on, moving ever deeper into the forest, the paint markers began to get lower. The farther in we hiked, the deeper the snow was becoming. We began encountering steeper areas and were starting to have some difficulty making it up the hills in our snowshoes.

After a couple of hours of strenuous effort, we reached a plateau. There was just one problem—we couldn't find the next tree marker. I looked at my watch. It was three-thirty. In the winter, darkness falls at four-thirty and by five it can be as black as pitch.

What were we going to do? It was too late to turn around. If we tried to backtrack, we would surely be over-taken by nightfall. This hike had taken a lot longer than we thought it would. And now here we were, out in the middle of nowhere, high up in the wilderness, with no marked path before us.

We spent most of the next hour trying to find a marker that would put us back on course. At first it was like a joke. We laughed at our situation. But as dusk settled our mood changed. Looking for a marker was becoming quite impossible. We realized we had gone so far into the forest that the snow line had actually risen above the paint markers on the trees, which were placed five feet above the ground.

It was now dark, and I mean *dark*. Have you ever been out in the middle of a forest at night? The only light you see is the moon and the stars, and that's if it's a clear night. We didn't know how far into the woods we had gone. In fact, we didn't know where we were. We couldn't have been too far from Frankenstein Cliffs, we thought. And, actually, that was a problem. You don't want to be near the edge of a cliff when you're stumbling around lost, cold, and tired at night in the forest.

Just the year before, during the summer, this same thing had happened to a couple hiking in these woods. They, too, were looking for Frankenstein Cliffs when it became dark. The husband took the lead, with his wife following behind. The darkness was so complete that they couldn't even see each other. They decided to each hold the other end of a long stick between them.

They had been walking this way for a while when the wife felt a sudden tug, and then the stick fell to the ground. She called for her husband. There was no answer. Terrified, she sat down and, for the remainder of the night, didn't move from that spot.

The next morning the tragedy became clear. Without even knowing it, her husband had walked off the edge of the cliff and plummeted to his death on the rocks below.

It was with thoughts like these that we decided our only option was to try to "bushwhack" our way out of the forest. We abandoned the trail (actually the trail had abandoned us) and began descending, we hoped in the direction of the highway.

We were experiencing great difficulty keeping our balance as we descended the steeply sloping gullies. We began falling down a lot. The hours of trudging through the deep snows were taking their toll on us. Each step, lifting our snowshoes high enough so we could put them down flat, was becoming more painful. We were exhausted, without food, except for one candy bar, and it began looking as if we would have to try to build some kind of shelter for the night. What would the temperature be this evening? Twenty below zero was not uncommon on a winter night in the White Mountains.

Just exactly where were we? Headed out of the woods? We thought so, but after a number of twists and turns, we weren't quite sure anymore. We were following whichever way went downward.

Wait. I thought I saw something. Was that a light in the distance? With all of these trees blocking the way, it was hard to tell.

There it was again! Praise God, something was out here. We became jubilant.

We had just been talking about how quickly hypothermia (rapid loss of body temperature) could, and had, claimed lives in these parts. A tired, wet, and cold hiker can expire in less than an hour when hypothermia sets in. You're really not aware of what's happening, and that's part of the problem. You become somewhat disoriented. All you want to do is lie down and close your eyes for just a few minutes. Yes, rest a little bit and then hit the trail again with renewed strength. There's just one problem. When you do close your eyes, you never open them again.

It wasn't at all uncommon to hear of at least one or two fatalities a year in the White Mountains. Most accidents occurred in the winter months. Occasionally we would read of some inexperienced hiker who would simply disappear and never be heard of again. In fact, many of the trails in these mountains were marked with signs saying, "Warning—this area has the worst weather in the United States. Only experienced hikers should attempt this trail, and only after registering with the AMC" (Appalachian Mountain Club).

Had we been lucky enough to discover some cabin out here in the deep forest? We didn't know, but for the next half hour or so that light shining in the distance was our connection with life. It was slow going. We were constantly losing sight of the light due to all the trees getting in the way. We would take a few steps, relocate the light, and then take a few more steps.

We were getting closer. Another few minutes and we would solve the mystery of this strange beacon.

Coming into a clearing, we found the light. There it was, a single bulb brightly burning high atop a telephone pole. There was no cabin or shelter in sight. But what we did see left us absolutely astonished.

Our eyes had been fixed on that glowing orb for the past thirty to forty minutes. And where had it brought us out to? The telephone pole holding this lamp aloft was less than two feet away from my car! We had miraculously found and followed this light right out of the woods to the very place where we had begun our journey all those long hours ago.

We were simply speechless.

This light had delivered us. Quite possibly it had even saved our lives. Could this have happened by chance? Was this just some incredible coincidence? You're lost in the woods, it's dark, you see a light, keep your eyes on it, and it brings you out to the very place you started from? Do you believe that?

As we drove home, a phrase kept repeating in my mind. It said, "Keep your eyes on the light. Keep your eyes on the light. No matter how dark it is, no matter how lost or hopeless you feel, just keep your eyes on the light and everything will be okay."

I've thought about this experience many times since then. I believe God saved our lives that day. He also gave me a valuable lesson about life from this incident.

Why were we saved? Because we saw the light and kept our eyes on the light. If we had remained looking at our circumstances, we would have remained in the dark. If we had gone with our feelings, we would have panicked. That light was our only hope. Interestingly enough, if it had not been for the incredible darkness, we might not have seen the light at all. You see, the darker it is, the brighter the light shines.

This is why we need to believe in and receive God's love on a daily basis. When we are surrounded by darkness, He is the light. God is the way through our trials. He shines the beacon that takes us out of the woods and into the clear. When we are lost, tired, and weak, God's light keeps on shining. Instead of cursing our darkness, we are far better off if we will look, and keep looking, to the light.

"Keep your eyes on the light. Keep your eyes on the light. No matter how dark it is, no matter how lost or hopeless you feel, just keep your eyes on the light and everything will be okay."

2

*W*hat *I*s a *W*ounded *H*ealer?

*N*ear the end of my live call-in radio program, "Let's Talk About Jesus," I announced that we had time for one more call.

A woman's voice came on the line. "Wayne, I've got to tell you what happened at your recent Carnegie Hall crusade." Her voice appeared calm, but her words trembled with emotion.

"My son had just gotten out of the Navy and was living with me here in New York. He never missed your radio program. When he heard you announce your crusade, he was overjoyed and asked me to go with him." She paused for a moment, as if gathering courage, and then went on. "One week before your service, my boy was mugged and stabbed to death. Wayne, my son loved Jesus with all his heart. At the funeral, I shared with our family about his last desire being to attend your crusade. Everyone was so moved by what I said that thirteen of our relatives, including brothers, cousins, uncles, and aunts, went with me to your service."

At this point in our conversation I commented that even in this painful period of suffering, loss, and mourning, God was doing a good work within her family. "Wait," she said, "there's more. When you gave the invitation at the close of your service for people to come forward and accept Jesus into their hearts, every single one of my relatives, all thirteen of them, got out of their seats and went up to pray with you."

Her voice was still trembling, but it was more joy than pain being expressed as she continued. "You wouldn't believe the difference in my family since that day. We're close to each other now. God's love has changed us all tremendously. I am actually able to thank and praise Him in all of this. Life truly has come out of death for my family."

While there may always be deep sorrow over the loss of her son, this dear woman's burden had been made significantly lighter as she saw the light of God causing "all things to work together for good" (Rom. 8:28).

As our conversation neared the end, I asked her, "If God had come to your son and said, 'You may live a long life, or you may come to Me *now* and through doing so bring thirteen of your dearest relatives to Me as well,' what do you think his response would have been?" Without a moment's hesitation she exclaimed, "Oh, I know. He would have chosen to sacrifice his life for the lives of those he loved most. Isn't this what Jesus did for us?"

Two years after our conversation, I received a letter from one of this woman's nephews, who had accepted Christ into his life at our crusade. He shared with me that both he and his brother, who had also responded at our altar call, were now studying for the ministry. So life continues to come out of death for this family and now also for the world around them. Out of this one precious grain of wheat that fell into the ground, a wonderful harvest is being gathered.

Was this woman some superhuman saint? I don't think so. She was simply a mother who loved her son. But through her tragedy, she witnessed a beautiful illustration of what happens when we choose, sometimes against all odds, to see the loving hand of God at work on our behalf, bringing life out of an otherwise lifeless situation.

Life comes out of death—this principle is at the very heart of the Christian faith. Indeed, this truth is seen throughout all of God's creation.

A tree dies and slowly returns to the soil from which it came, providing rich nutrients for new life to spring forth in the forest.

In the state of Washington, Mount St. Helens explodes with violent fury, leaving miles of blown-down trees and ash-covered earth. For the next year there are no signs of life. But wait—wildflowers are poking their way up through the dense ash. We see the tiny stirrings of a new ecology on this once-dead mountain.

A Canada goose stands between her young and any assailant, ready to give her life without hesitation in the ancient act of maternal protection.

If we have eyes to see and ears to hear, all of creation is proclaiming the truth of resurrection life.

The clear epitome of this death-into-life principle is found in Jesus. In Matthew's Gospel, Jesus said, "The Son of Man [a Messianic title] will be delivered to the chief priests and scribes, and they will condemn Him to death, and will deliver Him to the Gentiles to mock and scourge and crucify Him, and on the third day He will be raised up" (20:18–19). In these verses we see Jesus aware of the cross awaiting Him. More than that, though, these words reveal that Jesus' eyes were set not upon His impending suffering, but upon the inevitable resurrection that would follow, proclaiming His victory over sin and death.

Simply and paradoxically, death is a stage all things pass through in order to reach resurrection life.

We experience one kind of resurrection when we initially come to Christ, receiving Him into our lives. We are raised or born again (John 3:3) in our spirits when we open our hearts to Him. And because of Jesus, we have the sure promise of eternal life. When the day comes that we breathe our last, we will be ushered into the presence of God with purified minds and resurrection bodies (1 Cor. 15:42–44).

But until that blessed day arrives, life will continue to unfold itself in a series of death-into-life experiences. The tragedy for so many is that they won't look for the resurrection; thus they remain stuck in a death fixation. Maybe they've had it drummed into their heads for so long that they're no good, not lovable, hung up, messed up, and mixed up that they can't conceive of good coming out of bad things for them. For many of us, by the time we come to Christ, we've already had so much negative input thrown at us that it can seem impossible to believe anything good can happen, so we just naturally gravitate toward seeing the worst in everything. And there certainly isn't anything worse than death, is there?

Instead of seeing good coming out of adversity, we have been conditioned to avoid adversity at all costs. While I'm not advocating going out and looking for trials, I will say there is no way to avoid them. We all have tribulations in this life. The great challenge for us is whether we will stop running and learn to listen to our pain, or go on ignoring its voice.

Because most of us hope to live in a world without tribulations, we often wind up distancing ourselves from everyone and everything that we feel brings tribulation into our lives. Sometimes I think we spend the first half of our lives building up our walls and elaborate defenses, only to spend the remainder of our lives trying to figure out how to become free of them.

Jesus could not give us His own life until He experienced His own death. He willingly became a seed that, falling into the ground, sprouted back to life for Himself and for all who would come to Him.

This same pattern works itself out repeatedly in our own lives. We may gladly quote with Paul the triumphant words, "I have been crucified with Christ; and it is no longer I who live, but Christ lives in me" (Gal. 2:20). It's as if we wipe our foreheads and say, "Whew, am I glad that's over with!" We like the idea of being identified with Christ's death because we want to believe that He did all the suffering for us so we won't have to suffer at all. But Paul also said, "I do my share . . . in filling up that which is lacking in Christ's afflictions" (Col. 1:24). He even went so far as to say, "I die daily" (1 Cor. 15:31). Now wait just a minute, Paul! We want all mention of suffering to be in the past tense, thank you. Don't give us any of this "I die daily" stuff.

Have you ever looked at the paradox of accepting by faith your crucifixion with Christ as an event in the past, while at the same time recognizing a very real, ongoing crucifixion in your present life? The church seems, by and large, to have done a pretty poor job of reconciling these truths with each other. The result of this inability to see both sides of the coin of suffering ("we have died"/"we are dying") is witnessed every day in the lives of thousands of believers who are bowed down with guilt and condemnation. They are convinced that if only their faith were strong enough, they would be able to rebuke all trials and tribulations. Because they can't confess their way out of their suffering, they are convinced they've let God down. The truth is that God may be performing His most beautiful and loving work in their lives through their trials, but they can't see it. Because they believe all suffering is in the past (the "we have died" side of the coin), they look upon all misfortune (the "we are dying" side of the coin) as being of the devil. And if you conclude something is of the devil, you most likely are not going to look for any revelation of resurrection life within it.

While everyone may be feeling this inner conflict, we unfortunately remain silent most of the time, perhaps because nobody else is talking about it. We are all like Paul, "daily dying," but we go on saying, "Fine thank you," when asked how we are, for fear of being rejected or looked upon as being a failure.

This is why we so desperately need to see the fleshed truth of the wounded healer.

We need look no farther than the life of Jesus to discover the principle of the Wounded Healer. The Son of God came to set the captives free, heal the brokenhearted, and "proclaim the favorable year of the Lord" (Luke 4:18–19). In order to do this, He had to be wounded. The Bible says, "He was wounded for our transgressions" (Isa. 53:5 KJV). Why? Why did Jesus have to be wounded for us? Couldn't God accomplish the work of our redemption without subjecting His only Son to the horrors of the cross? Why did Jesus have to suffer in order to make us whole?

This truth of the Wounded Healer appears in the Bible as early as the book of Genesis. When God confronted the serpent in the Garden, after the fall of Adam and Eve, He said, "He [Messiah] shall bruise you on the head, and you shall bruise him on the heel" (3:15). It's generally accepted that the serpent God was speaking to was the devil. In this prophetic word the Lord foretold the defeat of Satan, "He shall bruise you on the head." But something else was revealed here as well. The phrase "you shall bruise him on the heel" indicated that while Satan would not triumph over the Messiah, he would, nevertheless, inflict a wound upon his adversary before his own defeat. In other words, Jesus was destined to be the Healer of our souls, but He would be a Wounded Healer.

I suppose God could have chosen some other way to save us if He had wanted to. But this was how He did it. We are forced to arrive at the truly amazing conclusion that Jesus freely chose to suffer for our sakes. The fact that Christ endured the cross and became wounded for our transgressions tells me a lot. I am convinced, nay, I know, that Jesus desires an in-depth intertwining of hearts with us. Through His manner of death I see that it's not merely an intellectual relationship God wants with us, nor is He primarily concerned with our theological confessions. His suffering was nothing less than His choosing to become completely identified with us. Our pain became His pain. Our burdens became His burdens. When Jesus died on our behalf, He shed real blood and suffered real wounds, all the time loving us.

This reminds me of the story about when someone asked Jesus how much He loved him. With a look of compassion in His eyes, Jesus said, "This much." And He stretched His hands out on the cross and died.

The writer of Hebrews, commenting on Jesus' suffering, said, "We do not have a high priest who cannot sympathize with our weaknesses, but One who has been tempted in all things as we are, yet without sin. Let us therefore draw near with confidence to the throne of grace, that we may receive mercy and may find grace to help in time of need" (4:15–16). The key to understanding the Wounded Healer is contained in this passage. Christ willingly suffered as we do in order that we may find mercy and help when we are suffering. This is the liberating truth of the Wounded Healer—our sufferings are not for ourselves but for others. Christ suffered for our benefit. In our own lives, if we are willing to accept rather than reject our trials and see them as not being against us but for others, then the door opens up for us to touch resurrection life in the midst of our pain. A wounded healer is someone who has suffered, but instead of being self-centered, the wounded healer sees suffering in an "other"-centered context. A broken heart is an open heart, a heart that can be filled with holy compassion and mercy for others, if that's what we choose.

Perhaps your response at this point is to say, "Okay. I can accept the fact that God was wounded for my transgressions. But didn't He suffer so that I wouldn't have to suffer?" The answer to that question is yes—and no.

In the sense that Jesus died for our sins and suffered for our rebellion against God, the answer is yes. You do not have to pay for your sins. Jesus paid the price in full. Once you receive Him as Savior, you are completely forgiven of all your sins. You will never have to pay any penalty or endure any punishment on account of them. This truly is amazing grace. So in this sense, Jesus did suffer on your behalf so you wouldn't have to.

But it would be a serious mistake to assume suffering will not be part of your Christian life.

Consider Paul. He didn't travel an easy road. Towards the end of his life, he was arrested in Jerusalem on false charges and spent the next two years in chains under house arrest in Caesarea. When the time came for him to be taken to Rome for trial, he had to endure a violent shipwreck (which we'll take a look at later on). As if this weren't enough, when he finally reached shore, shivering and soaked through to the bone, he was bitten by a snake as he gathered sticks to build a fire for warmth.

Paul was frequently thrown in prison. He was beaten with thirty-nine lashes on numerous occasions (the saying was that forty lashes would kill you). He was ridiculed by his own children in the faith. He was stoned and left for dead outside of Lystra. When he finally did have his trial at Rome, all of his friends, with the exception of Luke, deserted him. His converts in Asia turned against him. And tradition says Paul was executed by decapitation.

Was Paul some out-of-the-will-of-God apostate? No! We know he was a powerful man of God. The point I am making is, we can't look at the successes of Paul while ignoring the sufferings of Paul. To do this is to see only half of the truth. You can't separate the power and miracles from the sufferings and adversities of this great apostle.

Perhaps we don't consider Paul's trials because we don't want to think of our own trials as being part of the will of God for our lives. But I believe that through our trials God is inviting each of us to become wounded healers in the same way Paul and Jesus became wounded healers.

As we will see in later chapters, the sufferings Paul endured became the very means of God's powerful anointing in his life. In particular, we'll take a close look at Paul's second letter to the Corinthians. In this epistle, perhaps more than any other, Paul reveals his fears, doubts, agony, and ultimate triumph in Christ as he accepted the challenge to become a wounded healer.

Before he came to Christ, Paul was the chief persecutor of the church. He was personally responsible for the deaths of many believers. While on his way to the city of Damascus, with orders in hand to arrest the followers of The Way (the name given the early Christians), a bright light suddenly shone around him, literally knocking him off his horse. There, in the dust, God spoke and revealed Jesus, the Messiah, to Paul. Blinded by the light of God's presence, Paul was taken by the hand into Damascus where he waited and prayed for three days.

In that city lived a Christian named Ananias. The Spirit of God came to Ananias and told him to find Paul so that he might lay hands on him for the restoring of his sight. Understandably, Ananias balked at this word from God. After all, Paul's reputation as the great persecutor of the church was well known in Damascus. Ananias wasn't too thrilled at the prospect of presenting himself to the very man who had orders to arrest him. But of course Ananias obeyed God and went to Paul.

Concerning Paul, the Lord said to Ananias: "I will show him how much he must suffer for My name's sake!" (Acts 9:16). God wasn't planning on talking to Paul about the joys of the Christian life. Instead, He was going to show him the hard path that lay before him as a believer. But I must emphasize this: God's message to Paul was not the talk of some negative or sadistic defeatist. The opposite is the truth. This was a message of victory, of power, and of love. Paul may not have understood it then, but as he grew in God he learned that in order to give real life one must learn real life. And the place where we learn real life is in our own baptism of fire. Years later, Paul wrote in his letter to the church at Rome that he didn't even consider his sufferings worthy of comparison to the great eternal riches in Christ that his trials actually revealed to him (Rom. 8:18).

I don't believe Paul came to this awareness immediately. This revelation of resurrection life was developed throughout his years of triumphs and tragedies. I suppose we would like to think we know what we need. We may try to convince ourselves that only "good" things should happen to us. But what really is good for us? If God allows difficulty in our lives, is that necessarily bad, or is it good? Do we know? Perhaps letting Jesus be Lord means allowing Him to give us what we need, rather than our telling Him what we need.

In the words of an anonymous poem I came across a few years ago, I find the wisdom of God. If we are willing to let these verses become reality, we will soon begin seeing all things in the light of His goodness and graciousness.

I asked God for strength, that I might achieve . . .
I was made weak, that I might learn humbly to obey.

I asked for health, that I might do greater things . . .
I was given infirmity, that I might do better things.

I asked for riches, that I might be happy . . .
I was given poverty, that I might be wise.

I asked for power, that I might have the praise of men . . .
I was given weakness, that I might feel the need of God.

I asked for all things, that I might enjoy life . . .
I was given life, that I might enjoy all things.

I got nothing that I asked for, but everything I had hoped
    for.

Almost despite myself, my unspoken prayers were
    answered.

I am among all men most richly blessed.

How about you? Are you ready to accept the challenge
of allowing your trials to teach you the way of transcendent life in Christ? Are you willing to let God show you
the light within your pain? Are you willing to open the
door of your heart to the revelation of the Wounded
Healer? When you really think about it, what alternative
is there?

3

*W*aiting
and *A*cceptance

*C*an we go yet?" This must have been the fifteenth time Jesse had asked me that morning. We were staying in Bar Harbor, Maine, at an oceanfront hotel; my son, who was eight at the time, was dying to go "tide-pooling." The only problem was that the tide was high at that moment, so there were no tide-pools to explore.

I tried my best to convince Jesse that when the tide is at its lowest, that's the best time to go searching. But he only looked the more disappointed that we weren't going right then and there. I promised him that if we were patient we would be rewarded, but I don't think he believed me. Jesse wanted to explore tide-pools, and he couldn't understand why we had to wait.

Morning finally gave way to afternoon, and still we hadn't gone. Jesse moped around, and when I suggested we do something else while we waited for low tide, he stated in a flat monotone, "I'm not interested." At that particular moment, my son's one burning desire, indeed his reason to live, had become to search tide-pools.

At three in the afternoon, when the tide was at its lowest, I said, "It's time." By this point Jesse was in such a black mood that he almost did not want to go anymore; but I prevailed and brought him, sourpuss and all, to the rocky shore.

And what a time we had! We found rock crabs, green crabs, hermit crabs, a sea urchin colony, sea cucumbers, and many other fascinating creatures of the sea. Jesse was so excited that he could hardly contain himself. I was happy too, seeing my son's joy and delight in the discovery of nature.

This is what my son had really been after. He just hadn't wanted to wait for it. I knew that Jesse wanted to go tide-pool searching for the adventure and excitement of discovering living things. If we had gone earlier, when he had wanted, we wouldn't have found anything. Jesse, disappointed, would have concluded that tide-pool searching is "boring." When I had explained to him earlier in the day that if we went then, we wouldn't find anything, he had responded, "I don't care. I just want to go now."

As we walked back through Albert Meadow to our car, aglow with the thrill of our wondrous tide-pool adventure, Jesse took my hand, and looking up at me, he said, "Dad, I'm glad we waited, because this has been the best."

Have you ever thought about how much of our lives are spent in the act of waiting? From something as small as waiting in line at the grocery store to something as large as waiting for a tribulation to end, we spend a significant part of our lives waiting. I've come to believe that, to a large degree, our happiness and peace in life depends upon how well we have learned to wait. Life isn't only a matter of what we do; it's also our attitude about what we do. Many people never gain a healthy respect for the work of time in their lives. But I have found that the people who are the happiest and most peaceful are the ones who have accepted and understood the wisdom of waiting. The wait itself is an important instrument of growth in our lives, if we allow it to be.

My son's desire to search tide-pools coupled with his unwillingness to wait for the right time had only created suffering for him. He desperately wanted to go tide-pooling and was only growing increasingly disappointed and angry with me. I had become "the bad guy" who was making him wait. But afterward I wasn't the bad guy anymore—I had become the great and wise dad who knew just how to do things right.

We all experience suffering, yet we remain unwilling to accept suffering as part of God's loving plan of growth for our lives. Our motto seems to be, "There is no problem so big that it can't be run away from."

We are used to running from adversity. No wonder we don't even consider the possibility that our trials may be intended to give us valuable information about ourselves, life, and God. If we would only be willing to wait and to listen closely enough, we would hear our suffering saying, "Accept me and you will be healed."

Instead of learning from our suffering, we prefer to deal with our pain by finding someone to blame it on. Just like Jesse looking at me with a darkened countenance, we designate scapegoats for our troubles, thereby excusing ourselves from any sense of personal responsibility. It's like cursing at the chair you trip over. Friend, it's not the chair—it's you.

Why are we so prone to look at the darkness around us while ignoring the light altogether? If I had done that on my hike in the Crawford Notch, I probably wouldn't have made it through the night. The darkness was the problem. Looking at that wouldn't save me. Blaming my circumstances on my friends, the snow, or any other thing was not going to help me either. I needed to see the light.

Scapegoating is nothing but a dead end, yet it remains one of our favorite secret (and not so secret) pastimes. We Christians are particularly talented when it comes to scapegoating. Anything bad is blamed on the devil. And if our prayers aren't answered the way we would like, God is blamed. Problems in the church are blamed on the pastor or on whoever disagrees with us doctrinally. Problems in the home can be conveniently blamed on an unsaved spouse. Isn't this wonderful? We've taken scapegoating and made an art form out of it. Through blaming everything on everybody around us, we excuse ourselves from all personal responsibility for our lives. Unfortunately, in doing so we also close the door on the light of God.

In John's Gospel, Jesus said, "These things I have spoken unto you, that in me you might have peace. In the world ye shall have tribulation: but be of good cheer; I have overcome the world" (16:33 KJV). In these words Jesus clearly stated that we are bound to encounter trials and difficulties in this life, not in spite of our belief in God, but *because* we believe in Him. If we would only be willing to learn the value of waiting, our suffering could be lessened and, in some cases, eradicated.

We are of God, but we do still live in this world. As long as we remain on this planet, we can expect to experience tribulations. But as Jesus said, we should also expect to be of good cheer in them.

Why? Because Christ has overcome the world. His light has overcome the darkness. By choosing to place our faith in Him, we are choosing to see above and beyond our immediate circumstances. Believing Him means believing He is with us and in us at all times, working His character and presence into our lives through all our experiences. In this light all things must work together for good because He is there.

Not only has Jesus overcome the world, but as His children, He has incorporated us into His victory. "And who

is the one who overcomes the world, but he who believes
that Jesus is the Son of God?" (1 John 5:5). This verse is God
telling us in advance of our ultimate victorious outcome
in this life—not because of us, but because of Him. Here
indeed is something worth being of good cheer about.

If we have the courage to embrace our tribulations rather
than deny them or scapegoat them on everybody else, we
will bring understanding and healing to our innermost
being. The sun will shine for us sooner than if we were to
continue playing the projection and denial game. If we
ignore what our trials have to teach us, we set ourselves
up to keep on repeating them. We may be dramatically crying out "Why is this happening to me?", but if we continue
looking for someone or something to blame our difficulties on, we really aren't interested in the answer. If we truly
want to gain insight, then we must be willing to examine
the role *we* play in our trials.

I believe it's essential to acknowledge tribulations as a
real presence and an integral part of our lives; however,
let's be careful concerning how we accept this truth. The
temptation to fall into self-pity is very strong when everything seems to be against us. The "martyr" mentality ("Oh
well, I guess God just wants me to suffer; nothing good
ever happens to me") is self-destructive. It keeps us stuck
in our problems while blocking out the light of God altogether. In the martyr mentality you are resigned to suffering, but you aren't accepting of it. You don't learn from it,
you don't grow through it, you don't see above it, and you
certainly are not of "good cheer" in it. You simply feel sorry
for yourself and want God to feel sorry for you too. Acceptance is saying a humble yes to God and waiting for His
timing to work all things together for good (Rom. 8:28).
Resignation is acceptance without hope.

Personal responsibility may be a phrase we wouldn't
want to hear in the midst of our pain, but I am convinced
that this is what God is inviting us to accept in our tribu-

lations. Personal responsibility does not mean things are our fault. Personal responsibility means the willingness to trust God when all is dark. It means living in God in this moment. It means looking to change ourselves, rather than blame others. It means being a disciple.

How do we look at our trials? The decision is ours and nobody else's. We either choose to see the dark, or we choose to see the light in them.

I believe it is healthy to accept the reality of tribulations, but it is imperative that we see them within the context of God's love. The part faith plays is to keep our eyes not on our tribulations, but on Him. If we are willing to believe *all* of John 16:33 (including the "be of good cheer" part), then we will actively desire to see our difficulties from God's viewpoint. Instead of the old "Woe is me" feeling, we will now say "All things work together for good."

Choosing to see light rather than darkness releases you from being a captive of your negative thoughts. Saying no to scapegoating frees you from the bondage of a defeatist/victim mentality. Instead of seeing the worst in everything, you are now free to actively look for the good in things. Fear and frustration are gradually replaced by a peace-filled accepting attitude when you are willing to accept personal responsibility for your perspective in the midst of your pain.

In my own attempt to learn from pain and experience good cheer over tribulations, I have struggled to understand the *why* of suffering.

I referred earlier to Paul's saying he made up that which was lacking in the sufferings of Christ. While this idea may appear to be blasphemous at first ("You mean there's something Jesus didn't do?"), I believe a closer look at these words reveals the key to understanding the purpose of affliction in our lives.

What could possibly be lacking in Christ's sufferings? We speak of Jesus' death at Calvary as "the finished work"; in fact, He said, "It is finished" (John 19:30).

Christ's sufferings were complete, as far as our salvation goes. His death and subsequent resurrection opened the door for us to be one with Him, for now and all eternity.

However, Christ's sufferings were lacking in one regard. There is one thing Jesus left undone—our growth. This is our responsibility. Jesus is our light, our strength, our wisdom, our "present help in time of trouble," and so much more. But in practice, Jesus is only these things to us as we are willing to acknowledge Him. In progressing through our own sufferings, we are given the divine opportunity to be identified with Christ and His Spirit in His sufferings. Our afflictions, when humbly submitted to God, sharpen our spiritual senses; enlarge our heart, understanding, and compassion for others; and mark our spirit with His own nature. So the sufferings of Christ are lacking only in that we need to go through our own sufferings in order to become fully conformed to His image. It's that simple. We do our part by "filling up that which is lacking in Christ's afflictions" (Col. 1:24), not as a penalty or punishment, but for our own growth, maturity, and peace.

It has definitely been in my darkest moments that I have seen the light of God's love and power shine the brightest. I have come to believe that His light shines all the time. The question is not, "Does God care about me?" The real question is, "Am I willing to believe He cares about me?" Am I willing to wait for His timing? Jesus has done His part. He has given me all I need, but am I willing to actively receive His love instead of remaining stuck in self-pity? Am I willing to recognize God's purpose, ministry, and light in me in the midst of my sufferings? Each day, moment by moment, we are given the choice to look either to our God or to our affliction.

Throughout my seventeen years as a counselor, I have seen people's trials produce very different and sometimes completely opposite results. I have spoken with dear souls who have endured incredible suffering and yet, through their hardships, they have become more giving, sensitive, and joyful. Their experiences have actually brought out an inner beauty which they had been unaware of. Through their willingness to see God's purpose in their affliction, through "keeping their eyes on the light," they have been radiantly transformed into the image of Christ.

On the other hand, I have spoken with individuals who have gone through deep suffering and have come away from their experiences hardened, bitter, and cynical. Convinced that God has let them down, they conclude that He must be a liar or that He doesn't care for them as He cares for most of His children. They feel completely abandoned, and they won't forgive God for it.

Depending on our perspective, our trials will either soften or harden our hearts toward God and humanity. It is up to us, I believe, to decide which way we will turn. We can continue following the old pattern of fighting every setback, or we can choose to begin viewing our setbacks as steps forward.

In my counseling ministry I have seen many people come away from suffering with hardened hearts. These folks never saw the value of accepting their tribulations. Some were still feeling guilt for having trials. Others couldn't seem to focus on anything other than their pain. Still others had accepted some formula that said that if their faith was strong, they could "confess" certain Scriptures and their trials would disappear. Maybe they "naturally" assumed trials were bad and therefore should be avoided at all costs.

Those who refuse to see the value of suffering have no other option but to become hardened in their hearts. Every new act of affliction only indicates to them just how little God cares. Instead of walking in the light, they are forever projecting ahead toward the next disaster waiting to hit them. Instead of judging their experience on the basis of God's word and character, they have, unfortunately, judged God on the basis of their experience.

I've gone through a fair share of trials myself, and I expect I'll go through more. I've lost my temper with God a number of times in the past. In my pain I've had moments when I've told Him, in no uncertain terms, just what I thought He could do with His kingdom if this was the way He was going to treat me.

Someone once said, "It's no wonder God has so few friends: just look at the way He treats the ones He's got." However, I have also faced the fact that ultimately my anger with God was nothing more than my own refusal to see His light and wait for His timing. Getting angry with God was only another manifestation of my own refusal to accept personal responsibility for my perspective.

Perhaps all of us have experienced moments of despair when we felt that we couldn't endure one more setback or difficulty. In times like these, it's helpful to contemplate the sufferings of Christ for, as we saw earlier, one of the primary reasons Jesus willingly accepted His own suffering was so He could be sympathetic and merciful to us in our times of suffering. "For we do not have a high priest who cannot sympathize with our weaknesses, but One who has been tempted in all things as we are . . . Let us therefore draw near with confidence to the throne of grace, that we may receive mercy and may find grace to help in time of need" (Heb. 4:15–16). If we would only open our hearts to God instead of feeling like a failure before Him, we would realize He is the One who desires to help and love us through to the other side.

I'm not saying I look forward to suffering. It's not as if I can't wait for the next "lesson from God's furnace." I'm not some spiritual masochist (getting my kicks out of getting my kicks). I enjoy peace, and I look forward to heaven, where sorrow and suffering will be things of the past. But if we are going to truly live in God's peace, then shouldn't it be a peace that exists on the mountain of blessing as well as in the valley of the shadow of death? By seeing His light, regardless of our darkness, we do have peace, because it is Him we are seeing.

It's tough being in the midst of some trial—praying, fasting, trusting the Lord, and trying as much as it is within your power to live according to the will of God. You may be painfully aware of the fact that your strength is depleted. You know you need Him, yet nothing seems to happen. There's just this awful silence. In a time like that, it is pretty easy to get angry with God.

You may be screaming (within your heart, if not out loud at church), "I can't take anymore, God. Your Word says you won't give me more than I can bear, and I'm telling you, I can't bear anymore!" And all the while you feel as if God just keeps cranking up the temperature in your own furnace of affliction. One conclusion I've come to through my own trials is that what God thinks I can bear and what I think I can bear must be two very different things.

When we're in the midst of difficulty, we hardly ever know what is going on or what the purpose of it all is. It's often only when we are on the other side of suffering that we can look back and discover the life that has been made manifest in us, and through us, as a result of our tribulation. We may praise God when we exercise hindsight, but it's difficult to praise Him when we're smack-dab in the middle of some fire, calling out His name while He seems to have gone fishing.

But what if we were willing to see our difficulties in a new light, accepting rather than rejecting our trials? We would free ourselves from anger (at God, others, and ourselves) and fear ("What did I do wrong?" and "What will happen next?"). We would clear the air to see God with us and in us all the time. If we choose in our dark times to see God rather than our circumstances, we put ourselves in the best place to see His "mercy and grace to help in time of need." When we believe His goodness is constant, these present trials are transformed and empowered to shape within us the beautiful heart of a wounded healer.

Seeing God's treasure in the midst of our suffering develops increased compassion, desire, and wisdom within us to give to others in their suffering. This, in turn, brings deeper healing to our own hearts. As we see ourselves caring more for others, we catch the first glimpse of the rare joy that is ours in sharing the fellowship of Christ's sufferings (Phil. 3:10). As we find God's light in our darkness, allowing our afflictions to sensitize our hearts toward others in their pain, we may even actually begin thanking Him for our sufferings!

God gives us gifts in our adversities that we cannot receive any other way. In particular, the truth of the Wounded Healer can only be manifest in our lives through our own personal contact with suffering. To ignore the wisdom of our trials would be to ignore the very place of God's power in our lives. If we avoid our problems, we may as well avoid our emotional and spiritual development.

Have you ever noticed that we seem to be capable of extending compassion to other human beings only after we have gone through similar afflictions and misunderstandings? If we walk through this life oblivious to the voice of our suffering, steadfastly ignoring God's communication with us through our own times of pain, we gradually degenerate into insensitive, self-pitying cynics. Even worse, we may deny our darkness by focusing instead on the darkness in others, becoming self-righteous judges.

As hard as it may be to accept, I believe our pain and suffering is our link with humanity.

After all, why are we here? What is our ultimate purpose in life? Why are we Christians? Aren't we here to realize God as our life, and aren't we commissioned to bring this message of good news to this hurting and dying world? If our primary purpose is to live in union with our Creator, fulfilling the greatest commandment to love Him with all our heart, soul, mind, and strength, then doesn't it make sense that to love Him all the time means we must see Him all the time? John put it this way, "We love, because He first loved us" (1 John 4:19). In other words, we can't love God except as He loves us. So to see God's love all the time, regardless of our circumstances, is to enable ourselves to love God all the time.

However, as we look at this foremost command of God, let's not forget our secondary purpose. When Jesus stated that the greatest commandment was to love Him, He went on to say, in the same breath, "And love your neighbor as yourself."

We are not here only for ourselves. We live much of our lives for others and, paradoxically, it is in living for others that we find our own healing, fulfillment, and completeness. Only when we take ourselves off the pedestal can we discover ourselves. Jesus put it this way: When we lose our life for His sake we are actually finding our life (Luke 9:24).

As long as we live an "I"-centered existence, assuming that "I" should always feel good and have no problems, we deprive ourselves of the very peace, joy, and abundant life we want. Our "I"-centeredness only makes us rebel against every unpleasant circumstance. But by accepting all of life, trials as well as triumphs, we accept God's goodness on our behalf at all times and are therefore enabled and empowered to give God's goodness to others all the time. By giving our life away, we gain an understanding of our true life.

Have you had times when you've wanted to throw in the towel? Have you felt like giving up on Christianity? Maybe you've seen everyone around you rejoicing in their miracles while you wonder why nothing's happening to you. You know you love the Lord just as much as others do, yet you're coming up dry while others are having their faces blessed off. Life seems to flow everywhere else, but your desert just gets hotter and hotter. At a time like this it may be pretty easy to give up.

The paradox is, it's often not until we reach this point of hitting the proverbial bottom of the barrel that we finally break through the confining restrictions of our circumstances into the glorious awareness of our higher life in Christ. When we're willing to see God in our cross, that's when we begin taking the first baby steps of resurrection life.

From this point on, we know better than to select which Bible promises we want to believe. In accepting Christ's presence and treasure within our tribulations, we finally come to the place of resting and trusting in God's wisdom and care for us. By yielding ourselves to become wounded healers, we are content, knowing God will fulfill His promises perfectly, every time, on time, and *in His time* according to His love and care for our ultimate good.

Somebody once said, "Men would pluck their mercies green, when the Lord would have them ripe for us." That's us all right. We want our prayers answered right away. We assume we know what is needed, we tell God, and then we give Him about two seconds to produce an answer. If we don't see an immediate payoff, we begin complaining—just as my son was upset because he did not want to wait to go tide-pooling. We do the worst possible thing at that moment. Instead of looking for God's hand at work in our lives, we doubt Him and begin looking for someone or something on which to blame our "unanswered prayer." Inwardly we feel that God isn't living up to His end of the bargain. By thinking this way, we alienate ourselves from the very One who can help us.

How often have we failed to see God's love at work in our lives? We're quick to give up when it appears He is denying His answer. I no longer believe God delays His answers. I believe He goes right to work the moment we pray.

The problem is us. We're so convinced that we know what we need, how we need it, and when we need it, that we refuse to see any other thing than that which we have prayed for. If we would only take our eyes off our requests and focus on Him, we would be able to see Him ministering to us at the level of our deepest need.

Through the act of accepting our trials and waiting upon God in them, we are given an opportunity to become conduits of divine life. We're just human beings, full of flaws. But if we will allow it, these flaws can become avenues for the light of Christ to shine through us, granting light to others who are also in pain and in need of God's love.

And what greater gift could God give us than that of bringing His tender, healing love to others? If you care to see it, your suffering is nothing less than the answer to your heart's desire to be like Jesus.

4

Concealing
and Revealing

"There's its tail!" someone in the growing crowd ahead of me shouted. Walking up the stairs from beautiful Sand Beach (on Mount Desert Island) to the parking lot, I encountered an increasingly excited group of people. Their eyes were fixed on a point far in the distance. I turned to look as one person blurted out, "I see it too!" Boy, that really got everyone going. It seems they were convinced a whale was out there in the water. Sure enough, as my eyes followed the direction of the many pointing fingers, every few seconds I did see something big and black emerge from the waves.

One fellow toward the back of the group turned to me and quietly said, "I think it's just a rock." Having spent many years visiting this island myself, I assured him that it was a rock, but suggested we keep it to ourselves so the others could go home and tell all their friends about the day they went to the beach and were visited by a whale.

Perhaps because they had never been to Mount Desert Island before or were unfamiliar with the coastline, these people were sure they were seeing a whale. If they had taken the time to get a bit closer, they would have seen that it was just a rock. But because they were certain they were seeing a whale, they didn't think they needed a closer look. Also, I think, they really wanted to believe they were seeing a whale.

One of the sadder aspects for me in the counseling ministry is encountering an individual in deep pain who refuses to see anything other than his or her own point of view. I have, unfortunately, met many people who were simply not willing to consider anything other than what they already believe. Even if their own perspective of themselves and others is choking the life right out of them, they will refuse to accept any new information that will challenge their view of life. Just like the folks who were convinced that they were seeing a whale, these people are absolutely sure that they know all they need to know, no matter how self-destructive that "knowledge" might be.

Many people feel an intense need to have a clearly defined, cut-and-dried, black-and-white concept of life. I believe this arises from a deep insecurity. Some, recognizing that no such cut-and-dried option exists, give up that desire and accept the fact that life is filled with questions and the unknown. However, others, refusing to accept the existence of gray areas or unanswerable questions, mentally "batten down the hatches," putting all their energies into blocking out any new light that could alter their tidy definitions of the universe. It's a fragile and extremely limiting sense of security when a person believes he or she must have all the answers.

In this frame of mind it becomes deceptively easy to stop seeking after God. After all, if you think you have all the answers, why would you need to seek new answers? So instead, you settle for a textbook approach to life. You've probably heard the statement, "God said it. I believe it. That settles it." While this can be a wonderful affirmation of a simple faith in God, I've come to think that more often than not, what we're really saying is, "I've made up my mind, so don't bother me with any new facts." It's like we're saying, "That's not a rock out there. It's a whale. So leave me alone."

There's an odd-sounding verse from the Book of Proverbs that used to puzzle me. It said, "It is the glory of God to conceal a matter, but the glory of kings is to search out a matter" (25:2). At first glance, I thought this was a confusing and perhaps even frightening concept—that God's glory would be in concealing matters. After all, I was praying for God to reveal things to me, not conceal them from me. This proverb definitely flew in the face of what I wanted God to do for me. Wasn't life hard enough already without God further complicating matters by playing spiritual hide-and-seek with us?

If we're experiencing great pain and intense need in our lives, we don't exactly want God to be hiding His answers from us. Have you ever heard anyone testify in church about how happy they were that God concealed matters from them? "Thank You, Lord, for keeping me in the dark when I was desperate. Thanks so much for being completely silent when I was crying out for an answer."

However, throughout these past few years, I've slowly grown to appreciate this word from Proverbs. "It is the glory of God to conceal a matter, but the glory of kings is to search out a matter." I've come to believe God conceals things from us because, in order for us to grow, we have to realize that we don't have all the answers. God, in His mercy, deliberately puts us in challenging situations where our answers are woefully inadequate. It is in this act of recognition that we begin the search. Probably the first step

toward any meaningful personal growth is in our acknowledging our ignorance and need for God's enlightenment.
Until we know that we don't know, I think we just won't
search for Him.

Proverbs 25:2 gives us two sides of a coin: God's glory
in concealing matters, and a king's glory in seeking out a
matter. There is something about the process of seeking
that awakens us and sharpens our senses. God hides things
from us so we may receive the wisdom and blessing that
come to us in the act of seeking them out.

There is much we can learn through seeking. I think
seeking after God's truth is designed to humble our hearts,
and that's good. Gradually we realize the limitations of
our thoughts, and we see how self-serving our opinions
can be. If we really did have all the answers, knowing our
human nature, I'm pretty sure we would tend to be smug,
arrogant, and insensitive to the many needs around us. But
in realizing we don't have all the answers, we come face-
to-face with our spiritual poverty. It's like telling everyone, "There's a whale out there," only to later realize it was
just a rock. In this humbled state of admitting we don't
know it all, we are invited to begin seeking after God, and
He begins revealing Himself to us, a little bit at a time. It
is God's glory to conceal a matter because that's how He
calls us to Himself, giving us the unfolding revelation of
His love for us and for this world.

Never knowing exactly where or when we may find wisdom, we must look for it everywhere. Along the way of
our search, time and again, we are confronted by how little we know and how many issues there are in this life that
simply do not have ready-made answers. We realize that
our ideas about this world and how life "ought to be" don't
amount to a hill of beans.

I'm convinced God has designed things this way because there is something about the search itself that gradually brings us to a much greater understanding of, and a

deeper compassion for, human suffering. It is through seeking after God in this manner that we become "kings." Through having an honest seeking heart, we begin to act as kings when we see this world with the same compassion as our King of Kings.

Wisdom doesn't come easy. The funny thing about all this for me is that the longer I seek after wisdom, the fewer things I am sure of. It reminds me of when Jesus said, "Martha, Martha, you are worried and bothered about so many things; but only a few things are necessary, really only one" (Luke 10:41–42). I relate to these words because my own path over the past few years seems to have progressed from being sure I knew it all, to realizing I didn't know everything, to where I am now, wondering if I really know anything.

I think the "one thing" Jesus spoke of was Martha's need to know God. In our trying to know so many things, we often fail to know the One most important thing of all. I don't think my own religious opinions have ever truly helped me or anyone else, but knowing Him has made all the difference in the world. It wasn't until I found myself in situations where my presumptions and opinions were completely useless, that I realized the need to seek after the matters He had concealed. Now I thank God that He conceals matters, because in that concealing I reach the end of myself and learn how to truly seek after Him. In His concealing of matters and my subsequent searching them out, I have discovered His great heart of compassion for all people everywhere. By concealing matters from me, God prepared a way for me to be lifted above the realm of my meager head-knowledge into a more glorious awareness of Him.

God hides His answers for our lives because it is only when we come to Him, leaving our "knowledge" behind us, that we are able to think new thoughts and see in new ways. God desires to lift us up to His level, where He can give us His wisdom for our lives. Our opinions act like lead weights, holding us down and lulling us into thinking we already know what we need to know.

Until life teaches us otherwise, I think most of us will assume we are wise simply because we have hard and fast opinions about subjects. But wisdom is something that must be searched out. We don't just wake up in the morning with wisdom; it's gained through experience. Our opinions, if they do anything, actually keep us from desiring wisdom.

Our cut-and-dried ideas about life are often born more out of ignorance than knowledge. The less we know about an issue, the more opinionated we may tend to be about it. As a few-months-old Christian, having read the Bible through once, I developed dogmatic beliefs about almost everything. I knew when Jesus was coming back. I knew who "true" believers were, and I judged, unmercifully, all who didn't fit my description of spirituality. I had opinions about ministers. I had opinions about the Holy Ghost, prayer, healing, and "the lost." In short, I was sure I was right about everything, and anyone who disagreed with me obviously did not love the Lord as much as I did. However, as I've grown throughout these past twenty plus years, I've seen that, in every case, my opinions were born out of a combination of arrogance, insecurity, and ignorance. Ultimately, my opinions were keeping me from the very God I loved.

The first nine chapters of the Book of Proverbs speak exclusively about our need, above all else, to seek after wisdom. Solomon wrote, "How blessed is the man who finds wisdom . . . For its profit is better than the profit of silver, And its gain than fine gold. She is more precious than jewels; And nothing you desire compares with her. Her ways are pleasant ways, And all her paths are peace. She is a tree of life to those who take hold of her, And happy are all who hold her fast" (3:13–18). Oh, how we need wisdom! Wisdom teaches us how to live our lives in peace, balance, and happiness. The main challenge facing us, if we are truly desiring after wisdom, is to be willing to let go of our concepts about this world.

I remember once watching an old Tarzan movie starring my favorite Tarzan, Johnny Weissmuller. In one scene, Tarzan's chimpanzee pal had gotten himself caught in a trap. Someone had hollowed out a coconut and put a banana inside. The chimp found the coconut and reached his hand inside to grab the banana. But now that he had wrapped his fingers around the banana, his fist was too large, and he couldn't remove it from the coconut. Tarzan's little friend was trapped. Of course all he had to do was let go of the banana and he would be free, but he wanted that banana, so he remained stuck.

This is what our opinions do to us. Our own ideas are like that banana. If we would only let go of them, we would be free. But we want that banana, so we refuse to let go. Consequently, we get neither the fruit nor the freedom.

If we are truly wise, we won't think of ourselves as being wise. We will know we are ignorant. And that's wisdom! Solomon said, "The beginning of wisdom is: Acquire wisdom" (Prov. 4:7). In other words, if you want wisdom, then the way to begin is to realize you don't have it.

The great storyteller Anthony de Mello told of a man who, desiring to be enlightened, went to see a spiritual master. When he was ushered into the master's presence, the man said, "O wise master, show me the way to true enlightenment." The master responded, "Go stand outside and lift your arms toward heaven." The man dutifully did as he was told. When he came back the next day, he said to the master, "I did what you told me." The master asked, "What happened?" The man replied, "Nothing happened. I stood outside through a torrential downpour and felt like a complete fool." "Well," the master thoughtfully said, "That's quite a revelation for one day, isn't it?"

To realize we are fools is a wonderful revelation, for then we can begin earnestly seeking after God.

Often when people first come to the Lord, it seems as if miracles are hanging like ripe fruit on a tree, just waiting to be picked. But because God is dedicated to our growth, the time comes when, in love, He stops spoon-feeding us. It's like a young eagle being ejected from the nest by his parents because it's the only way he'll learn to fly. If we have a desire to be more like Jesus, to have a heart for God, and to be ministers of His love in this world, then we will, at some point, be ejected from our nest so we may begin our lifelong search for wisdom.

How does God call us to this quest? I think about the only thing He can do is to conceal matters from us, so our opinions will fall flat. Our old dogmatic attitudes, the ones we used to thank God for, gradually become more and more like a giant straitjacket, allowing no room for growth or environment where we can ask the questions we need to ask.

I'd like to share a story with you of one person's search that brought her out of bondage to her own opinions into a glorious and love-filled freedom in Christ. This woman's journey led her from a place of self-assured and close-minded misery into a compassionate and appreciative understanding of life. I want her to tell it to you in her own words, so I'm printing the letter she wrote me in which she detailed her own quest for that matter which God had completely concealed from her:

Dear Wayne,

    I have gone through a five-year process, based upon my inability to forgive my ex-husband. He was a Spirit-baptized Christian who divorced me and remarried within six weeks!

    In my self-righteousness, I entered into a zealous ministry against divorce and remarriage, shouting "Adultery! Adultery!" all the way.

Although I forgave them both, as many as seventy times seven every day, I could not overcome my ill feelings. The guilt on my own soul (of unforgiveness) kept me bound up and miserable. My will forgave, but my heart remained bitter. I cried out for release, but could not find the root of it.

After four years of struggling, I finally sold everything I owned, pulled up stakes in Michigan, and moved to Atlanta. With a resentment against God that I denied, I proceeded to take up my own life and make my own freedom.

The doctrine against remarriage had literally imprisoned me in the hopelessness of a life alone. I had only seen God blessing my "adultering" husband and his wife. I decided God did not punish adultery, so I went back to the life I had once abandoned eight years before.

I dove back into the nightclubs, the drinking, and the sexual sins. The "freer" I got, the more bound up I became. Alcohol sank its hooks into me again, and so did sexual lust.

I finally cried out to my Father to come and rescue me. I was broken, bruised, ashamed, and very repentant. In His wonderful mercy, my Shepherd came to me in my cliff-hanging state.

He now had my attention. I realized that there dwelt, within my own heart, the capacity to rebel against God in the very same areas I had so haughtily preached against. I had demanded judgment in others' lives, for their sins, and here I was in my pain and anguish, doing the same things I had condemned. I felt just like Peter when the cock crowed three times.

Almost immediately I found myself in a bizarre situation. I became very attracted to a married man (a Christian brother) who was separated from his wife.

This man's character and personality were uncannily like my ex-husband's. He told me there was another woman in his life. By this time I had heard his whole sad story, and I was puzzled at my compassion for this situation. His story was the same as my ex-husband's. But now I was seeing his side . . . and feeling his pain.

As I gave him my testimony (the wronged wife), he was intrigued. Because of my love, he listened, and God was able to get through to him.

I was, of course, convicted of my initial interest in this man, and I repented of my feelings towards him. However, through this whole process, the Lord began to work in my heart in regard to His mercy and love for (yes, even) unfaithful husbands who divorce their Christian wives and remarry again! Had I not realized the true condition of my heart, I would have risen up in indignation, and I am sure I would have lashed out at this man. I would have quoted every Scripture on divorce, remarriage, and adultery that I had memorized for four-and-a-half years. Can you imagine what would have happened if God hadn't changed my heart?

But now I knew that I, too, was capable of the very same things. I, too, had run headlong into sin, and when I was lost and without hope, God reached out to me once again. Through His immeasurable mercy and forgiveness I was restored. The beauty of it all (which still astounds me) is that God did not condemn me. Believe me, I knew my sins all too well. No, He loved me, He cared for me, and I was renewed.

So, instead of judging this man in the midst of his own anguish, I gained his confidence. I simply pleaded with him, in love, and prayed for God's mercy on him, and that's what turned him around.

After much prayer, in which I sought God for the reason all this had presented itself to me, the dawn began to break. I came face-to-face with my own bitterness towards those who had hurt me. As I was confronted with my feelings, the Lord superimposed my compassion and understanding for this man over that of my ex-husband and his wife! For the first time I saw what had held me prisoner for so long—my own bitterness and unforgiveness. God had graciously forgiven me of all my sins, but just like the unforgiving servant Jesus spoke of in Matthew 18, I had still been unwilling to extend God's forgiveness to those who had sinned against me.

There was a new heart beating within me now. I knew I would never again overestimate or take confidence in my own spirituality. At long last, through much pain, failure, and frustration, I had found the mercy of God. I knew I could never again go back to my old self-righteous, condemning ways. This former "prophetess" had been humbled by her own weaknesses.

I thank God for replacing my stony heart of judgment with His heart of love and compassion. I am reaching out in love, and I am seeing hearts turning to God. What a difference mercy makes!

Enclosed is a poem the Holy Spirit inspired me to write as a landmark. I could only be set free through mercy—my own mercy toward others!

Mercy Rolled Away the Stone

I harbored a dark and deadly sin
In the tomb of my wicked heart.
A sin that kept me paralyzed
In grave clothes from the start.

The sins against me, I retained
But they held me to my debt.
I wasn't able to forgive,
So how could I forget?

For years on end I struggled,
Trying so hard to be free.
What I held onto so tightly
Had a stranglehold on me!

I held a man to keep his vow
And blamed him for my plight.
For whatever ills life had for me,
I was blameless in my sight.

Through misery and poverty
And guilt upon my soul,

I wandered through the wilderness
And lost all self-control.

My unbelief grew ever strong,
While faith was laid to rest.
Finally death caught up to me,
And God put me to the test.

With darkness all about me,
And the smell of flesh in death,
I knew I couldn't save myself
From this tomb that took my breath.

Then I heard a shout, calling my name,
And quickly realized
That the voice I heard was Mercy
And it opened up my eyes!

That's when Jesus let me see
The reason I'd been dead
Was the absence of *my* mercy—
I had played the judge instead.

So, Mercy rolled the stone away
And commanded that I live,
For without mercy I was doomed to die
And was helpless to forgive.

R., 8-24-85

This dear woman's story is a wonderful example of how God concealed a matter and then, in love, let His daughter search it out. What God had concealed was His mercy. This sister was sure she was right in her attitude against her ex-husband, and she used the Bible to back up her opinions. But she was also emotionally imprisoned by her bitter heart, which she denied.

Through her own experiences, God drew her to the awareness of her need for mercy. She wasn't aware she needed or lacked mercy until she came face-to-face with her capacity to disobey God. It was then that she gave up her opinions and saw how destructive they had been to everyone, herself included. By seeing her own need for and response to mercy, she was liberated from the prison she had built around her life. Mercy set her free.

Perhaps you feel God is concealing some matter from you. Maybe you're staring at a trial or injustice and can't see any redeemable purpose in it at all. You might even feel as if you are being abused by God. Maybe you're watching others being blessed while your own faithfulness seems to be yielding precious little.

I encourage you to believe God is nurturing you, calling you from the deepest part of His being to search for Him. In the final analysis, I believe God hides His most precious treasures within life's most difficult trials. Because He loves us and cares so much about our own welfare and peace of mind, He draws us out of our pain to seek after Him. In the presence of His mercy and unfailing love, we are lifted up out of ourselves and are set free in the awareness of His heart of compassion. There our hearts are humbled before Him, and we begin finding our own healing. We become partakers of His divine nature (2 Peter 1:4), aware of our King's heart, when we search out those things that He has concealed from us.

Yes, it is the glory of God to conceal a matter, but it is for our great glory and eternal benefit that He invites us to search out that matter. And as we continue our search, we find Him, we find our own true selves, and we find His heart of compassion for all of life.

5

The Lesson
of the Seagull

This was going to be the fulfillment of a long-standing fantasy.

For years I had been vacationing just off the coast of northern Maine on beautiful Mount Desert Island. Acadia National Park, the second most visited national park in the United States, draws more than two million people annually to this modest twenty-mile-long island. Acadia has it all—stunning pink granite coastline, sparkling saltwater beaches made from crushed seashells, quaint fishing villages, freshwater lakes and beaches, mountains, carriage roads, hiking trails, and abundant wildlife. Simply put, Mount Desert Island is a nature lover's paradise.

I had been told that the scenic shore road, which meanders along the most magnificent section of coastline on this island, was ideal for cross-country skiing. For the last couple of years, I had brought my skis with me whenever

I visited Mount Desert Island during the winter, but I was always disappointed. Either there was no snow on the ground or what little snow there was had been frozen solid.

But this year I finally hit the jackpot. I had come here for a few days to pray and to prepare myself for an upcoming teaching seminar. I couldn't have asked for better skiing conditions. A few inches of newly fallen snow lay glistening on the ground. It was mid-January, and I had been lucky enough to come during a rare midwinter thaw. The temperature was in the thirties—a real heat wave! Not a cloud was in the sky, and the absolutely brilliant sun caused the ocean to sparkle like a multitude of diamonds on the waves. I imagined that everything looked almost as if it had just been created by the hand of God moments ago.

I could dress lightly today. No need for any stifling thermal underwear or the scratchy wool shirts I usually wore when out in the woods during winter. No, today all I needed was my vest, unzipped, over a cotton flannel shirt.

I parked my car near the shore road and proceeded to check my backpack. Let's see—books, Bible, journal, mandolin (yes, it fit right in there), some fresh bread, cheese, and my wineskin (filled with my current favorite—natural apple-raspberry juice). Everything was there, and I was ready to go.

I put on my gaiters. These handy little items covered my ankles and kept the snow out of my boots. And I slipped on my special cross country gloves. The top sides of these thin gloves were vented with air holes, so they could "breathe." After only a few minutes of skiing, even in sub-zero temperatures, I would work up a pretty healthy sweat. The worst thing to do, when exercising outdoors in the winter, would be to wear garments that wouldn't breathe.

Okay, my skis were on. I skated a few paces, dug my poles into the fresh fallen snow, and away I went.

What a glorious day! The "clang, clang" of a distant buoy

could be heard over the sound of the gentle ocean swells kissing the rocky coastline. An occasional seagull drifted by, scanning the waters in search of food. A solitary cormorant dived under the surface, came up a minute later, regained its breath, and dived again. If this wasn't paradise, I surely couldn't imagine anything more beautiful.

With the ocean on my left and gently rising Gorham Mountain on my right, I skied up the shore road into a rich green forest of fir trees. Numerous deer tracks could be seen in the snow as I pushed my way up the slight incline toward Otter Cliffs. This particular place on Mount Desert Island is the highest section of Atlantic coastline north of Rio de Janeiro. I paused to rest as I reached the top of these cliffs, which plunge more than seventy-five feet straight down into the ocean.

I had gotten warm. Taking off my vest, I unstrapped my skis and sat on the pink granite retaining wall with my Bible in hand. From this spot I could see back down the coast I had just skied. In the distance lay Sand Beach, with the curiously shaped, and appropriately named, Beehive Mountain to the left and one of my favorite hiking trails, Great Head peninsula, to the right.

I read some Scripture while absorbing the sun's rays, which made it seem much warmer than it was that day. As I often do when communing with the Lord out in nature, I took out my mandolin and began playing. Sometimes I like to improvise, or make up music on the spot. It's kind of like singing a worship song to God that only He and I will ever hear. That's what I was doing and I was truly being lifted up and blessed as my heart overflowed with His Spirit. What a great combination—worshipping a wonderful God and beholding His magnificent creation all at the same time.

During this period of spontaneous worship, I noticed a solitary seagull, slowly drifting toward me on the air currents.

In fact, quite a wind had kicked up. As it came in off the ocean, I could see the trees bending under its force. An occasional crow came scooting by, propelled forward by the strong breeze. All the while this seagull didn't seem to be moving a muscle. It just kept drifting toward me effortlessly.

Wait a minute! How could this gull be floating toward me, when the wind was blowing against it? This seagull should have been riding the current away from me, not toward me. What was happening here?

My attention became completely fixed on this bird. I noticed other gulls, furiously flapping their wings as they attempted to fly into the wind. It didn't work. One by one, they gave up. They would peel off to one side, and when the stiff breeze grabbed them, they were quickly whisked away out of sight. But this single gull I had been watching for a few minutes now just kept drifting on. How long had it been since this seagull had flapped its wings? How was it able to come toward me, against the wind, while all the other birds had been exerting their full power and had failed?

As I sat there pondering these questions, I had an inner feeling that there was something important for me to see here. Then I felt the Spirit of God speak to my heart. Here is the gist of what I remember His inner voice saying to me that day: "The difference between this bird and all the other birds is that the others are fighting the wind, while this gull has learned how to submit itself to the wind. By yielding to its power, rather than resisting its power, this seagull has learned how to ride the wind. This bird has a different 'attitude.' Its body is positioned so that this contrary wind, which is beating back the others, is actually being used to propel this seagull forward. By passively accepting the breeze, this gull is going places where the others, with all their effort and straining, can never go."

As I reflected on these words, I realized that in my own life, I had more often than not been just like the gulls fighting the current. When adversity descended on me, I had the unfortunate tendency to resist it with all my strength. Trials were to be endured, not enjoyed. They were certainly not looked upon as vehicles by which I could move forward. Yes, I really was like those fighting gulls.

Could it be possible that, just like this lone seagull I had been watching, I too could discover a way of accepting my own "winds" and in doing so, learn to ride them instead of resist them? After watching this scene for a while, I decided I wanted to be like the gull yielding to the current instead of those fighting against it.

And just as this gull had changed the attitude, or position, of its body, angling itself so that this adverse wind was actually put to work *for* it, perhaps I too could change my attitude—inwardly. Maybe if I were willing to look at my own winds as a help rather than a hindrance, I could learn to rest instead of wrestle in the trials of life. If I sought to understand the wind instead of rebuking it, praying for it to end, and quoting Scripture verses against it, maybe I would find God making the wind work for me instead of against me.

On this magnificent winter's day, as I thought about this visual lesson unfolding in the air before me, God showed me the way by which I could learn, as it were, to go with the flow. The wind was exactly the same for all these birds. So the wind was not the problem. The problem was in the attitude of the seagulls. All the others were the same, but this one gull had changed. Rather than being at the mercy of this gale, this particular bird had learned how to take advantage of the contrary wind. In a sense, it dared to be different, to break out of the pack mentality, and in doing so, it learned how to fly in the face of adversity without moving a muscle.

What did I do with life? When I could smell trouble in the air, I would brace myself and expect the worst. In the midst of my own winds of adversity, I would question where I had gone wrong, or I would think of someone to blame. In general, I felt fairly miserable during trials. Trying to keep my faith intact and my eyes on the Lord was about the best I had learned to do so far. Beating my wings and going nowhere would be a fairly accurate way of describing how I often felt when surrounded by my own tribulations.

To see adversity as a means by which I could grow and move forward—that was a new concept. I knew that because of Jesus I was "more than a conqueror," but I thought this meant I would make it through to the other side, maybe just barely. I pictured this as more or less painfully enduring one blow after another, hanging on by my fingernails, while God dragged me, kicking and screaming, through my tribulations. I believed I was a conqueror because of Jesus, but I guess I saw myself as just barely conquering, if at all, when life would smack me around.

Was it possible to do more than just endure? Was being of good cheer in my tribulations more than just seeing a light at the end of the tunnel? Was God calling me to actually dive into the winds with a new attitude and to see these adverse conditions become the very means by which I could learn to fly like a gull?

As I reflected on these thoughts in prayer, I knew this was exactly what God was challenging me to do. As long as I continued seeing trials as being "bad," I would forever be at their mercy. I would try my best, but it would really be no more than flapping my wings against a power greater than myself. I would get nowhere.

But what if I were to position myself differently? What if I changed my attitude? What if I could begin to look at trials as being (gasp) good for me? What if I even came to look at adversity as my . . . friend? If I were willing to accept tribulations instead of fighting them or flying from them, perhaps I would see how to let their power work for me. If a seagull could do it, why couldn't I?

I had gone out that day to do some skiing, but God, in His wonderful love, taught me how to fly.

6

Accepting Your Humanity

*H*ave you made peace with yourself? Are you comfortable with your humanity, or do you struggle, seeing yourself primarily in terms of your failures, flaws, and shortcomings?

One of the things I admire most about the apostle Paul is that he seemed to be right at home with his humanity. Here's a man who wasn't afraid to be transparent. He said what he felt, and he didn't seem to worry about how others took his honest confessions. When Paul was sick, he said, "I'm sick" (Gal. 4:13). When he was afraid, he said, "I'm afraid" (2 Cor. 7:5). When he was weak, he said, "I'm weak" (1 Cor. 2:3). When he was depressed, he didn't hide that either (2 Cor. 7:6). Paul wasn't giving ground to the devil or cancelling out God's power by the honest admission of his true emotions. God is a lot bigger than that anyway. No, Paul was just being real.

Maybe I relate to Paul so well because in his letters I see a man like me—with weaknesses and fears. Paul even confessed to encountering a despair so deep that he wanted to die (2 Cor. 1:8). In a strange sort of way, I find comfort in the knowledge that this man who loved God so much, who was used by Him so powerfully, could at the same time be dealing with the emotions I deal with on a fairly regular basis.

Paul wasn't one of these always-on-top-of-the-mountain characters Christian biographers seem to be fond of writing about. Paul was a real man experiencing real problems. Through these problems, he tells us, he discovered the key to resurrection life. We ought not ignore the fact that in Paul's mind, his sufferings were the very avenue to his power and effectiveness as a minister of the gospel.

In reading Paul's letters I see a man who truly understood God, yet at the same time experienced doubts and fears just like the rest of us. If anything, Paul appears to be quite at ease speaking of his weaknesses. I believe one of the main points (if not *the* main point) in his second Corinthian letter was to openly reveal his humanity for the benefit of these young and immature Corinthian Christians.

Jesus was always at the center of Paul's writings. But in this particular epistle we see Jesus, the Treasure, presented within the context of Paul, the earthen vessel (4:7). I think the confessional tone of this letter was deliberate so that others might more readily recognize Christ within their own humanity. The beauty of 2 Corinthians is not so much Paul's honest acceptance of his humanity, as refreshing as that is, especially in this day when we Christians are so accomplished at hiding from our own humanity. No, the real beauty of this letter lies in Paul's discovery of God's blessings actually coming to him through his humanity and weaknesses.

Like Paul, I know I'm just an earthen vessel. He wrote, "We have this treasure in earthen vessels, that the surpassing greatness of the power may be of God and not from ourselves" (2 Cor. 4:7). This passage of Scripture deeply ministered to me a few years ago. I had been feeling pretty low. I was down on myself, examining my Christianity and concluding I was a royal foul-up. Have you ever felt that you had two left feet, spiritually speaking? Well, that's how I was feeling.

Anyway, I felt impressed in prayer to turn to this passage of Scripture from 2 Corinthians. As I was reading these verses about the treasure in the earthen vessel, I felt the Spirit of God speak to my heart, saying, "You would like to be perfect, wouldn't you?"

"Yes, Lord," I responded. "You know this is what I want, to glorify You in all things." I thought God would be pleased with my reply.

"There's just one problem," His inner voice continued. "If you were perfect, I couldn't use you."

"What? Why is that, God?"

"It's simple," He explained. "I am your treasure. I live inside you. Now, if you are perfect, you are, essentially, an earthen vessel without any cracks or blemishes."

"Sounds good to me, God."

"It's not as good as you think. You see, there's only one way people can see the light of the treasure, and that's if the earthen vessel containing the treasure has cracks in it. A perfect vessel shines its own light and hides the light of the treasure altogether. But a cracked, imperfect vessel lets the treasure's light be seen by all."

"Wait a minute, God. Do you mean it is through my imperfections and weaknesses that you are seen in me by others? Are you saying my faults are really assets to you?"

"Think about it. Do people relate to someone who appears to be perfect, or do they more readily relate to someone like them, someone who struggles with the same problems and questions as everyone else?"

"Well, I guess you've got a point there."

"Here's what I'm telling you. Instead of hating yourself and agonizing over your every weakness, I say accept your humanity and realize when you are weak you are in the perfect place to see Me shining through you. I made you the way you are. If I had wanted you to be faultless, I could easily have created you that way. But if I had, you would not depend on Me and you would be insensitive to others in their pain. No, it's someone who is aware of his imperfections that I can use best. I challenge you to see Me in your weaknesses. If you will do this, you will soon be thanking me for the very things you have hated yourself for."

This is the gist, or what I remember, of this time of illuminating dialogue with God in prayer. So I'm now happy to tell you that I'm a cracked pot for Jesus. Don't get me wrong. I desire to be obedient, and as much as I am able, I am obedient. But now, instead of mentally whipping myself for having faults, I thank God for His love. Instead of looking at my darkness, or cracks, I look at His light shining through my cracks, and in that act I am lifted out of myself into Him. Because of this, I have been brought to a place where I have at last made peace with myself and can thank God for my humanity.

We're all earthen vessels. I've got my cracks, and you've got yours. However, according to the Bible, our cracks aren't the issue. We all possess our own unique flaws and imperfections, but the point is, we have a treasure shining within us. So what are we going to look at, the earthen vessel or the treasure? I don't know about you, but I've discovered that seeing the treasure shining through my cracks is a lot better than just looking at my cracks and agonizing over them.

When Paul says, "We have this treasure in earthen vessels," this is a glorious revelation, not just some ho-hum theological fact. It's important to recognize that Paul had stopped looking at his flesh as if it were some major stumbling block to his faith. To the contrary, Paul was brought to the startling conclusion that God was even there, in his flesh, revealing His goodness, love, and commitment.

Can you believe this for your own life? Are you willing to see God in you, as your treasure, at all times? It's fairly easy to sense His presence and approval when we feel as if we're walking in His Spirit. But what about the times (the many times) when we feel as if we've totally missed the boat on spirituality altogether? What about when we're fouling things up, when everything goes wrong, and when we know we're not in the mind of Christ? Are we willing to see God loving us and manifesting Himself at those times?

If it is true that God can and does come to us through our weaknesses, then why does so much of today's Christian teaching focus on denying our humanity, as if to say it is a bad or evil thing? Instead of recognizing and accepting ourselves, we are all too often made to feel that *we* are the problem. We must totally deny ourselves, even our own personalities, if we are to be holy.

I must confess my own concern that much of Christian teaching today just does not have the ring of reality to it. Most of the messages I hear revolve around what we *should* be like or how things really *ought* to be. It's as if we are convinced that the only way we can be acceptable to God is if we become absolutely perfect. And, unfortunately, we assume perfection comes when our own self or personality ceases to exist.

I remember being in a worship service once where the minister spoke quite honestly and candidly about his own ups and downs as a Christian. The congregation didn't know what to do with this openness. Noticing their obvious discomfort, this minister paused and said, "I'm not telling you the way it ought to be. I'm telling you the way it *is*."

Isn't it a relief to know that the Bible tells us the way it is and not just how it ought to be? I'm glad the great heroes of the Bible were also ordinary human beings with human weaknesses. Look at David. He was a murderer, an adulterer, and a liar. Yet the Scriptures testify of him, saying David was a man after God's own heart (Acts 13:22). Peter denied Jesus with loud cursings, yet this was the man who later on became the leader of the Jerusalem church. Paul used to kill Christians, yet God chose him to take the gospel to the Gentiles. I figure I'm in pretty good company with these characters. I can relate to them. I experience the same kinds of feelings they did. I love God like they did, but I can also mess things up. If God could use them as they were, then I am confident He can use you and me the way we are.

Why do you think people keep listening to messages that do nothing but tell them they're not good enough? Why do people keep going to services where all they get is another earful of spiritual putdowns? They're always being told that if they really loved God then they would do this or that. Why do people choose to live in a world where "ought to" is the governing principle? Could it be that most people have been convinced that they are, in fact, no good? Perhaps they have been led to believe that the only way God can love them is if they finally arrive at that fabled place of sinless perfection.

Are you willing to accept the truth that God loves you just the way you are, complete with warts and pimples? Or do you feel as if you're never good enough? Do you think the only way God can love you is if you strive toward the so-called goal of becoming the perfect Christian? Perhaps you're thinking, "If I try hard enough and deny myself long enough, one day I will arrive at the place of sinless perfection and then I will be confident God loves me."

Ah, yes, the perfect Christian. We all know this person, don't we? At least we think we know this individual. The perfect Christian is never down, never angry, never fearful, always strong in faith, and always in the midst of some personal, ecstatic revival. Is this what you believe you ought to be?

There's only one problem with all of this. I have never met this perfect Christian. And I have yet to meet anyone else who has found this perfect Christian either.

I have met many who desperately want to believe they are perfect Christians. These people are really in trouble. Unable to accept themselves as they are, they constantly deny their own emotions. Afraid of any feeling within themselves that might be considered "unholy," they, in fact, hate themselves and conclude that God hates them too. Believing their acceptance to God is based on their flawless performance, they pretend to be perfectly happy and always on top of everything. It's as if they hope to fool God in the same way they fool themselves.

These poor Christians are to be pitied above all others, for they are forced to live a life of double standards. The more they pretend to have it all together, the more their inner cauldron of self-hatred is stirred up. Instead of being lifted up to God's level where love rules, they have dragged Him down to their level where insecurity and denial are center stage.

These dear souls need to know they are loved by God, right now, as they are. They need to see that their humanity needs to be accepted, not denied. In short, they need to receive Paul's revelation of the treasure in the earthen vessel.

This is why we need the fires of affliction in our lives— to burn all the phony baloney right out of us. Once you've personally gone through the unpleasant experience of feeling like your head is in a vise grip while God turns up the blowtorch on your backside, you find this refreshing encounter has a remarkable way of freeing you from theorizing about how things "ought" to be. None of the simplistic, one-sided formulas do a bit of good when your life is falling apart. You can smile all you want, and say "Fine, thank you" to everyone who asks how you are, but you won't be one step closer to any meaningful life as long as you continue in your performance as "the perfect Christian."

Theories evaporate pretty quickly when you are in the furnace of affliction. But I believe it is the grace of God allowing you to go through the fire, for it is in the furnace that you discover One walking with you "Who looks like the son of God" (Dan. 3:24–25). Indeed, God may never be so real to you as when you find Him in your own furnace of affliction.

I would love to tell you that it doesn't have to be this way, but sometimes it's not until we are in the midst of tribulation that we are willing to pay attention long enough for God to show us what is real. Why? Well, most of the time God can't get through to us until we are forced to let go of our sacred formulas and ideals. And only in the midst of great tribulation are we willing to examine and challenge those precious assumptions that may have, in the final analysis, deprived us of so much life in Christ.

Each of us experiences trials and conflicts. Are we going to continue playing the game of denying the existence of these things in order to try to live up to some fantasy of the perfect Christian, or are we going to admit that suffering is a large and important part of our existence? We can go on squandering our time, hoping for a painless and problem-free "Disneyland" type of life; or we can start living abundantly right now in the midst of our pain.

Your problems will either be your enemy or your friend. The decision is up to you. I encourage you to exchange the destructive posture of looking at life in terms of what you think *should* be, for a realistic appraisal of what *is*. If you will believe that God loves you all the time everywhere, then you will start appreciating His great work in you through your own apparent weaknesses and flaws.

Wouldn't you like to be in the position of seeing God's covering on the whole of your life—good times and bad? Don't you want to be free of the guilt-producing conclusion that God must be rejecting you when things go wrong? How would you like to see His love at work in you just as powerfully in your darkness as any other time? If you will take the step of accepting, even embracing, your humanity, I believe you will soon be realizing all this and more.

In 2 Corinthians, Paul admits to having deep-seated fears. He confesses to going through times of great despair in his Christian experience. Paul believed in keeping a good confession. He realized the importance of seeing God over all, and in all, of his circumstances. But he didn't make the mistake of denying his inner fears and doubts, as if ignoring them would make them go away. Paul had a bigger revelation of God than that. He knew God's power wasn't found in formulas or in the denial of his so-called negative emotions. Paul knew the power of God came out of His heart of love for us.

Beginning his letter, Paul wrote, "Blessed be the God and Father of our Lord Jesus Christ, the Father of mercies and God of all comfort; who comforts us in all our affliction so that we may be able to comfort those who are in any affliction with the comfort with which we ourselves are comforted by God. For just as the sufferings of Christ are ours in abundance, so also our comfort is abundant through Christ. But if we are afflicted, it is for your comfort and salvation; or if we are comforted, it is for your comfort, which is effective in the patient enduring of the same sufferings which we also suffer" (2 Cor. 1:3–6).

On the rational level, these verses make no sense at all. For if God is so merciful, why doesn't He stop our suffering? If God is so great, why doesn't He just comfort us and skip the affliction part? Why not get a big blessing from God, saving us from pain, and let us share that with our brothers and sisters? Why do we have to be hurt in order to make others feel well? Is this any way to treat your children, God?

When we read the Bible as if it were only a rule book on the Christian life, we will never be able to touch the beautiful truth contained in these verses. However, if we are willing to come into the spirit of the Word and see the omniscient love of God being poured forth in these Scriptures, we will not only have a new vision for our own ministry to those who are hurting, but we will also have the question of our own personal suffering answered. Instead of denying all unpleasant experiences or rebuking them as if they were a curse from the devil, we will be able to embrace our trials as channels of God's healing power and anointing in our lives.

Here's what I think Paul was saying: "You know, I really praise God, because the afflictions I go through, the sufferings I endure, are not really for my own sake. They are for you! I see something happening in me when I suffer. I see myself being broken down. I see myself not being able to trust in my own faith or my own Christianity. I see how much of a failure I am. I see Paul, the major Christian flop of the century. I recognize how miserably faithless I can be. But do you want to know something? God loves me anyway! He comforts me anyway! And so, my brokenness becomes life for you. Through my trials, my heart is enlarged. I have found, in the midst of my sufferings, that I have something to give you. Through my afflictions, I have discovered the always-abiding, unconditional love of God. I want to give this love to you, so that when you go through your own valley of the shadow of death, you will fear no evil because you will know His love is with you. He is with you all the time. If you will let Him, He will actually use your pain to increase your knowledge of His love within you. How can I be sad when I see the beautiful gift God has given me to give to you?"

In these moving words we see the heart of a wounded healer. Here is someone who underwent constant tribulation and yet continued to exemplify such a beautiful life.

The depth of Paul's pain was surpassed by the tender love, which he allowed that pain to produce in him. Because he chose not to harden his heart toward God, Paul was freed to see Jesus' love and purpose being fulfilled in him through his sufferings.

Paul actually discovered joy in his trials. His afflictions became the very vehicle by which he soared into heavenly places. In the midst of his tribulations, Paul received the glorious revelation of the true nature and care of his Lord. This higher reality brought Paul to the place where he was able to proclaim: "Most gladly, therefore, I will rather boast about my weaknesses, that the power of Christ may dwell in me" (2 Cor. 12:9). We'll take a closer look at this verse later on.

This certainly is a far cry from the type of Christianity that equates being an overcomer with being on top of every situation in wealth, health, and prosperity. Instead of looking for the glory of God on the other side of our mountain of tribulation, perhaps we too should have the courage to see God's glory right now, in the midst of our trials. Could it be that God has been here all along, and we haven't seen Him? Have we been looking so intently at our problems that we have missed the tender hand of His love, caressing our hearts and souls in Him?

Maybe, just maybe, if you'll stop hating yourself, stop despising your weaknesses, and stop running from your humanity, this is when you will be able to see the presence of God in you—in all of you. By accepting your humanity, you may well discover you are accepting the Spirit of Christ into your life.

7

Springs in the Valleys

*Y*ou don't find water on the mountaintop. For that you have to go down to the valley.

During one of my outdoor worship times not too long ago, I came across Psalm 104, a beautiful piece of Scripture that speaks about the glorious wonders of God's creation. Reading through this Psalm, I found one verse that stood out: "He sends forth springs in the valleys; They flow between the mountains" (v. 10). Although these words refer to nature, they also contain a key truth for our spiritual lives. The nourishing springs are found *in the valleys*, flowing between the mountains. They're not *on* the mountains but *between* the mountains.

We often speak of "mountaintop experiences" as those times in our lives when the peace of God prevails, when there are no problems. Everything is going great, and we're only aware of the blessings of the Lord. But there are valleys, aren't there? There are valleys so deep that all of the blessings you rejoiced in yesterday are nowhere to be found today.

Each of us experiences both valleys and mountains in our lives. Some people spend more time in the valleys than on the mountains, and that's okay. Real life is lived out in the valley. Don't get me wrong; I love being on the mountain, rejoicing in all the Lord's blessings and goodness. But when I hear the call of Jesus to pick up my cross and follow Him, He usually leads me into the valley, because that's where the hurting souls are, the souls He has come to set free.

In my early days as a Christian, I viewed life in terms of the way I thought it ought to be. I'd reason, "The Bible says this, therefore things ought to be like this." My idea of how things ought to be, unfortunately, had become more important to me than the needs of those living in this world without the knowledge of Jesus Christ. In a way, my dogmas had become like a biblical fairy tale that I subscribed to. My Christian universe was black and white, and if your life fell into a gray area or didn't fit my beliefs, then I was sure you had to be out of God's will. Living according to the way things ought to be, I discovered, actually hardened my heart against any person or experience that did not fit my preconceived and (I now recognize) narrow-minded view of life.

It's fairly easy to piece together a belief system, choosing arbitrary Bible verses that shore up our ideas while at the same time failing to get an overview of the whole of Scripture. We can become so entangled in the business of propagating our doctrine that we may forget what the central message of Christianity is all about. Luke's Gospel says Jesus came to earth to "seek and to save that which was lost," but all too often our faith becomes a theological insulation against the very world Christ died for. In other words, we can be so caught up with loving God that we may forget that God loves people and has asked us to do the same.

That's pretty much where I was in my spiritual infancy. There were no valleys for me. No, sir. I was God's soldier and I was going to walk on the mountain all the time—in Jesus' name of course. My dogmatic allegiance to the Lord actually isolated me and inhibited me from growing in a love and acceptance of people, because it was my faith that was most important to me, not the cries of the lost. I was more interested in figuring things out than in reaching out.

About the only thing you can do if you come across someone like I was, is to give him time. Everyone can live on the mountain for a while, particularly if the mountain is based on theory rather than reality. Some even try to prolong the "mountaintop experience" by going into denial when the mountain becomes a valley. They say, "This isn't a valley. That's what the devil wants me to think." It's as if we refuse to believe any pain or suffering could come our way if we are truly walking in the Spirit of Jesus Christ.

But I have found the ministry of the Holy Spirit to be most valuable and precious when I approach life *as it is*, and life consists of mountains and valleys. Maybe you think you ought to always live on the mountains. Well, God bless you, but life-giving springs are in the valleys. To live only on the mountain would be to miss the balancing work of God's Spirit in our lives. God lets us go through valleys because there we find the opportunity to take the blessing of the mountain and find a real-life application for it. The valley experience refines the mountain experience.

God "sends forth springs in the valleys; they flow between the mountains." Have you experienced this pattern in your life? It happens constantly in mine. It is almost as if we have to reach a certain point of brokenness before a particular issue of life can start to flow. There's something about being in the valley that either breaks us, shakes us, or wakes us. Then, all of a sudden, we discover the life of God in a very sweet way in our darkest place. It's not that our Creator is sadistic. God doesn't get a kick out of sending us into the valleys, but in His love and commitment to us, He allows those valleys because that's where we often have our most blessed breakthroughs.

But what happens when we're having a "valley experience"? We usually try to figure out what we did wrong. We assume God is punishing us. But this narrow perspective misses the greater reality of God's work in our lives. Valleys are a natural (and necessary) part of our existence. God doesn't create our valleys, but He does create His goodness in them.

Valleys are transformed into mountains when we learn to see the life of God within them. Finding the spring of living water in your valley is the same as finding the key that unlocks the door to your next mountain. We rejoice on the mountain for a while, enjoying that present moment until the next valley comes along. But just as the Bible says, "Darkness and light are alike to Thee" (Ps. 139:12), our valleys and mountains are also alike to Him. God reveals precious truths to our hearts in both experiences.

Once, while visiting Acadia National Park in the winter, I had a similar type of insight from nature. Walking through newly fallen snow one day on the Wonderland Trail on the south side of Acadia, I was thinking about how great it was to experience this island in such solitude. I seemed to have the whole park to myself. This place could get very crowded during the summer, but now in the winter it was bleak and deserted.

While in this contemplative mood, I felt God challenge me. The impression I got from His Spirit went something like this: I enjoy this island more than others simply because I love this island. The weather is secondary to me. Others come only in the summer because the weather is primary to them. To me winter and summer are the same because I just love being here. Thanks to this attitude, I can enjoy this beautiful spot year-round, whereas others may only enjoy it for a short season.

This is where the challenge came in. I felt God nudging me to look at my life in the same way as I saw this island. In other words, if I would love life itself, and not just life in the "summertime" (when all is well or when I'm on the mountain), I could be joyful all the time—and not only for a short season.

I'm still learning the wisdom of God's lesson to me that day. Of course I still prefer the mountaintop, but I have learned my most profound and life-changing lessons in the valley. I may have learned to praise God on the mountain, but I've learned to truly appreciate Him in the valley. I've learned to love God on the mountain, but I've learned the depth of His love toward me in the valley.

As a new Christian I believed that if I did everything just right and if my obedience to the Lord was 100 percent, God would always keep me on the mountain. But over the years I've been learning that God's top priority with me is my growth in Him. God has always come through for me and led me in His victory; but He rarely, if ever, has done it the way I thought He should or would.

I used to assume that being in a valley was the same as being in failure, but I now believe valleys are nothing less than opportunities for God to reveal His goodness to us in a tender and intimate way. The difference between a miserable valley and a pleasant valley is whether or not we are willing to drink from the springs of God in them. To me, this is the spring—consciously depending on and drinking in the lovingkindness of the Lord in those dark moments. As David once wrote, "Even though I walk through the valley of the shadow of death, I fear no evil; for Thou art with me" (Ps. 23:4). Sometimes that's the whole point of being in a particular valley, that we might realize God's presence with us.

As a young believer experiencing his first few valleys, I gradually came to realize that much of my rebuking the devil and confessing the Word had more to do with a denial of reality than a faith in God. As I grew in the Lord, I learned more and more how to, as Paul said, "be content in whatever circumstances I am" (Phil. 4:11). However, even though I was developing more of a consciousness of Jesus Christ with me in the valley, I would still dread the next valley that might come along, so I still wasn't getting the point.

Today, in my walk with the Lord, I'm simply at peace with God—whether I'm in the valley or on the mountain. If I've just come out of a valley, I rejoice in that time of peace, but I'm not chewing my fingernails worrying about when the next valley might come along. The mountaintops are beautiful, but I've discovered the valleys are beautiful too, because God sends forth springs in the valleys—springs of living water. There's something about being on the mountain that makes us think we've had something to do with it. But when God's hand feeds us in the valley, we know it's all His doing. That alone is a tremendous revelation.

The Scripture says God has commanded that "Light shall shine out of darkness" (2 Cor. 4:6). Sometimes it's not until we're in the valley of intense darkness that we are finally able to see the light of God shining. If life is easy, we might not see God's light because, in a way, there's light all around us. But go into a time of darkness, and we'll find ourselves able to keep our eyes on the light of God like never before. There's nothing like being in the dark to make us truly appreciate God's light.

I believe both valleys and mountains are needed in our lives. I don't go looking for the valleys, but they do have a habit of showing up. I don't rebuke them, condemn them, run from them, or deny them anymore. I am content to know that "The Lord will accomplish what concerns me"—a great promise from the Scriptures (Ps. 138:8).

So, whether you are on the mountain or in the valley, I encourage you to rejoice and rest in Him. If you're on a mountaintop, thank God for the view. If you're in the valley, thank God for the spring He's sending forth. Either way, you're a blessed person because God is taking every experience in your life and using it to draw you to Himself and to bring you into a greater awareness of His power, presence, and wholeness at work on your behalf.

8

What about Faith?

What a beautiful sunny day! Joe stepped out his front door only to find his neighbor Fred on his hands and knees in his yard. Being a friendly type of guy, Joe asked what Fred was doing. "Looking for my keys," Fred growled. Joe immediately joined his neighbor in the search.

After they had covered the yard for the third time, Joe said, "Gee, Fred, are you sure you lost your keys out here?"

"Oh, no," Fred answered. "I lost them somewhere in my house."

Stopping everything, Joe exclaimed, "Then why are we looking out here?"

Fred grinned and simply replied, "Because it's brighter out here, that's why."

Within many hearts there beats a strong desire to believe that if our faith is just right and if we maintain the proper confession, God will reward us by steering all difficulties out of our path. We want to believe this, but there is just one problem—it's not true.

I'm not saying there aren't folks who preach precisely this type of theology. There are, and part of me would like to believe what they say. Sure, I'd love to believe that all we have to do is push the right Scripture button, with the right amount of faith, and God will automatically zap all trials out of our way.

But this is like looking for our keys where we haven't lost them. If Fred had really wanted his keys, he should have looked in his house. However, he preferred the bright and warm light outside, so he kept looking and obviously came up empty. This is what we do when we ignore what the Bible says and instead choose to believe what we *want* the Bible to say. As long as we try to make Scripture fit our ideals and desires, we too come up empty when we try to make our principles work in the face of life's ups and downs.

Perhaps you're thinking, "Well, why do so many preachers say we can and should avoid pain? Why do they say it is our right as God's children to be excused from all suffering and sickness, if our faith is properly maintained?"

Ministers who adhere to this "no-more-suffering" theology are most likely avoiding the reality of their own pain. I remember listening to a particular radio teacher once who constantly preached that all sickness was of the devil. He authoritatively taught that Christians who know how to confess the Word would never be sick, poor, or depressed.

On this particular day, the minister's voice sounded different. He was terribly congested. It was evident in every word he said that he had a severe cold. Near the end of his broadcast, he finally declared, "The devil is trying to make me believe I have a cold, but I am not going to receive that lie."

Now tell me, who was the one lying here? Who was the one being fooled? It was obvious to me that this man had a cold. Whether it was from the devil or from just being human, I don't know. But I do know he had a cold.

Is God honored by this type of "confession"? It seems to me that Jesus had something to say about the truth setting us free. I believe this minister and his listeners would have been much better off by looking reality square in the eye. Perhaps God would have been more honored if this minister had assumed responsibility for taking care of his cold, along with looking to God in faith and prayer. If I fall down and cut myself, I'm not going to pretend my cut doesn't exist. I think God is more pleased when we make use of that highly underrated spiritual gift of "common sense."

Perhaps some ministers, like this man, haven't yet learned to accept their humanity. Maybe they expect flawless perfection of themselves. If they do, you can be sure they are going through a tremendous inner battle. They have to figure out how to hold onto their ideal, while at the same time being faced with their obvious failure to live up to that ideal.

In a scenario like this, a minister can wind up absolutely hating himself. He thinks he has a handle on the truth. He believes it. He preaches it. He tries to live it. But he fails; he always fails. He must either revise his theology or pretend his failures don't exist, because they're too painful to look at.

The Bible says, "Love your neighbor as yourself." But what if you hate yourself? What if you think you're a horrible excuse for a Christian? You might start projecting your inner anger onto others. Because you despise yourself for not living up to your ideals, you start hating everyone else too. After all, you reason, you're really trying. So if you are miserable, then everybody else should be miserable too. In this environment you can easily fall into the sin of judging all those who don't seem to be trying as hard as you are. In this twisted theology, you may actually wind up condemning many happy and contented Christians.

Preachers caught in this emotional vise can become so busy projecting guilt and condemnation upon those around them that they never slow down long enough to take a good hard look at the harmful and unrealistic theology they have created. In their desire to live in a world without suffering, they actually create suffering for themselves and for everyone who listens to their messages.

Here's the rub. You may listen to these messages and hear that if you keep all your doctrines in letter perfect order no bad thing will be able to touch you. Then you look at your own life and say, "But bad things *do* touch me." If you are honest with yourself, you know your faith is not 100 percent all of the time. So you conclude your problems exist because your faith isn't strong enough. No matter how hard you try ("I've named it, claimed it, stood on it, rested in it," etc.), you just don't seem to be able to cast the spirit of tribulations out of your life. In the end you are completely frustrated, down on yourself, and out of touch with God's love. You figure He's disgusted with you. Instead of depending on His unconditional love and power working in you, you feel as if your deliverance and well-being are totally dependent on the confession and maintenance of your faith. And all the while these preachers just go merrily along, keeping their "good confession."

I urge you not to fall into this trap. Have the courage to accept the truth that the Christian life has many trials. This was the honest message that the apostle Paul preached, that we enter the kingdom of God "through many tribulations" (Acts 14:22). Accepting God's hand and purpose in the midst of our trials is not nearly as painful as believing all trials are of the devil and should not touch us in any way.

I remember a call I once received on my radio program from a woman who was terribly distraught. Because she was so emotional, it took a while to piece her story together. Here is what had happened.

Having recently come into the Christian faith, this woman and her teenage daughter had joined a church where the "positive confession" principle was strictly adhered to. No "worldly" doctors for this crowd. No, sir. These folks weren't namby-pamby Christians. They took God at His word, or so they thought (they took the words of God that shored up their beliefs, while ignoring those Scriptures that would balance or refute their beliefs).

After this woman and her daughter had been attending services at this church for about a year, the daughter became seriously ill. Instead of calling in a physician, the church rallied around the family. It was clearly a moving experience for this woman. Parishioners were bringing groceries, cooking meals, helping with house chores, and of course regularly confessing this girl's complete healing.

What a testimony this was going to be, they all thought. Souls would surely come to Christ as a result of this miracle of healing. Everyone was positive that the healing had, in fact, already taken place. Their job, they supposed, was to maintain the faithful confession until the healing actually manifested itself.

All the while, this young girl's condition deteriorated. But people thought there was no need for concern. After all, wasn't this just like the devil, to make them doubt the power of God? No, this congregation was steadfast, and although this woman thought a doctor should be called, she was counseled to stand firm in her confession and not "give ground to the enemy."

The girl died.

This grief-stricken mother was upheld during those first difficult days by the love and constant support of her church family. They were with her every moment, caring and consoling her in the Lord.

But, after a few weeks, there was an apparent change in the church's attitude toward this poor woman. The pastor let it be known that God was not pleased with the way things had turned out. This girl should have been healed. Instead she had died, and somebody was to blame.

It couldn't have been the pastor, because he knew he had enough faith to heal this girl. No, the finger was clearly pointing to the girl's mother. Despite her confession, it was becoming obvious to the church that her faith must have been lacking.

A delegation was sent to the woman's home to confront her with "the truth" of her failure. She was told, in no uncertain terms, that the reason her daughter died was because she didn't have enough faith. Yes, in their minds they were fully convinced that it was the mother's fault.

This poor testimony, this apparent lack of faith, simply could not be condoned or tolerated by this church. After all, they had a reputation to maintain in their community. After deliberating and seeking God's will, they decided to "discipline" this woman by excommunicating her from their assembly. She was kicked out of their church, and in a very short while was remembered as the woman who had let her daughter die because she didn't have enough faith.

As I listened to her tragic story, I tried to comfort this woman as best I could. She was in terrible agony, and her pain was not going away.

At first she lived under a cloud of despair. She had let her child die. She felt she was no longer worthy to call herself a Christian. She hated herself.

Gradually she came to her senses. As she read the Bible, she discovered that this "positive confession" theology was not taught in the Scriptures. Paul admitted to being sick (Gal. 4:13). Timothy had a stomach problem and was even advised to take wine for his ailment (1 Tim. 5:23). How unChristian! Paul wasn't advocating that Timothy merely trust God for his healing, but he was actually encouraging the use of man-made means (wine, no less!) to make Timothy feel better.

There was Epaphroditus, who became sick to the point of death because of his Christian service (Phil. 2:25–27). Then there was this startling statement made by Paul in his second letter to Timothy, "Trophimus I left sick at Miletus" (4:20)! Luke, Paul's closest friend and the author of our third Gospel, as well as the Book of Acts, was a doctor. And he didn't even publicly renounce his profession when he came to Christ.

In addition, a closer reading of Jesus' parable of the good Samaritan revealed that it was the despised Samaritan, not the religious priest or the Levite, who was commended. And what did this Samaritan do? He bound up the wounds, provided medicine (oil and wine), and took care of the injured man in this story.

These observations did not heal this woman's pain, but at least she was now able to separate the destructive theology of this church from the true teaching of God's healing power and love.

As our conversation ended, it seemed that this dear sister was comforted as much as she could be at the time. Her grief would remain, but she was now freed from thinking her daughter had died because of her lack of faith. With this burden off her back, she was able to behold Jesus' comfort, care, and complete love for her.

In the midst of this terrible tragedy, God graciously allowed this woman to become a wounded healer. To me, this sister had great faith. She was willing to see through the pain and the false teaching into the truth of God. Her faith had held her together through this period of darkness. Another person might have thrown in the towel and given up on God altogether. But this precious saint kept on believing. As far as I am concerned, this woman possessed a faith that far outshone the superficial "faith" expressed by the church she had attended.

Instead of being consumed by bitterness, this sister allowed her anger to go to the cross. In its place she discovered a compassion for others who were hurting. Resentment would have turned her inward, where she would only see how unjustly she had been treated. Instead, she reached outward with courage, faith, and love. She humbly allowed God to use her to counsel and comfort others in their own pain and grief. Through many tribulations, this woman had entered into the kingdom of God in a greater way than she had ever known.

Coming into the awareness of the wounded healer is one of the best things that has ever happened to my spiritual growth. Before understanding this truth, I was constantly agonizing over the "Why" of trials and afflictions.

Your first contact with the truth of the wounded healer may be dismaying. But after you get over your initial shock, you may find great comfort, life, and love in acknowledging and accepting your wounds. Seeing God's higher-life purpose in our wounds is the beginning of healing for those wounds.

If you are going through any trials or suffering at this moment, I pray you will choose to believe God means it to be life-giving for you. No matter what situation you find yourself in, God desires to manifest His own character and nature in you through it. Seeing this truth frees you from looking at your problems and being overwhelmed. Maybe it's time to let go of the idea that you ought to be able to confess your way out of your difficulties.

Your wounds are nothing less than instruments of healing love. Recognizing this work of God in your innermost being will surely bring you to the place where you will want to comfort those around you, in their pain, with the same comfort God has shown you in your pain!

It is through the valleys that we come to the very heights of heaven. As that great preacher of a former era, C. H. Spurgeon, once said, "Many men owe the grandeur of their lives to their tremendous difficulties."

If someone approaches you with a deep trial or wound in his or her heart, and if you haven't been through your own dark night of the soul, you may not be able to relate to that individual at all. Perhaps the most you would be able to offer would be the standard platitudes and pious-sounding sayings. "Just trust in God, brother. Keep hanging in there. God will come through for you. You've got to have more faith. Keep a stiff upper lip." I'm sure you've heard them all. These are well-meaning words but they are usually said by those who have no idea what an individual is going through.

Even worse, if we deny or reject our own suffering, we can easily wind up playing the guilt and projection game with those who are admitting to affliction in their lives. We say, "I have never had that problem, so something must be wrong with their faith." If we dump that on those around us who are hurting, then we will have actually dealt with a wounded brother or sister by wounding him or her even further.

But in accepting our own suffering, we are enabled to bring the healing balm of love to those who are trying to deal with their own wounds. Before we become wounded healers, we tend to look more at our personal belief structure than at a person's pain or true need. But once we have been dragged, kicking and screaming, to the slaughterhouse of the Lord, where our precious and unrealistic ideas are put to death, we find that what we thought would kill us is, in reality, the one experience that has actually brought us out of death into the resurrection life of Jesus Christ.

From this point on, we may find ourselves hesitant to speak our own minds. We may come to loathe our own opinions and first impressions. Instead of reacting with judgment, we may now discover ourselves feeling the hurts and pains of those around us. We may be surprised to find ourselves weeping with those who weep and rejoicing with those who rejoice (Rom. 12:15). Through our own afflictions, Christ's heart of compassion is awakened within us.

The days of handing out narrow-minded dogmatic formulas will be over. In their place will be a new desire and inner compulsion to minister God's tender love, encouragement, and compassion. Within our love, encouragement, and compassion, the people we help will see a revelation of Jesus Christ. Our own personal wounds make us healers. Seeing others receive life through our wounds will, in turn, bring greater healing and life to our own hearts.

Ultimately, we will thank God that, through our own weaknesses, failures, and tribulations, we have been brought to the place where we are able to feel another's pain. Our newfound desire to love others will definitely overshadow the suffering we've gone through (and grown through) in order to come to this new awareness.

Do you recall the Scripture where Jesus said we would do even greater works than He did (John 14:12)? Why do you think Jesus said this? What did He mean? Doesn't it almost seem to border on blasphemy to think that we would do greater works than Jesus? At first glance this verse just doesn't seem right. We know God is infinitely greater than we are. He's not in need of any help from us. Yet Jesus made this amazing statement.

The meaning of this verse comes into focus as we begin to understand the principle of the wounded healer. If God wanted to, He could send ten million angels to earth today to preach the gospel to every living creature. He could unleash a barrage of miracles so powerful that no one would be able to doubt His existence any longer. God could do this, but He doesn't. Why? Because He has chosen another way.

He has chosen to use us.

You can argue with God all you want about the wisdom of His decision, but sooner or later you will realize why He has chosen to use us to preach the gospel to the world.

In order for the world to see Jesus in us, which is what it will take for any worthwhile revival to happen, we must first become conformed to His image. It is through our own sufferings that this conforming takes place. If the Bible says Jesus "learned obedience through the things which He suffered" (Heb. 5:8), then how can we hope to learn obedience in any other way? Yes, God could preach through angels and miracles—and our lives would not be personally transformed one bit if He did this. But because He loves us so much, He has chosen this way—the harder way, the longer way, but also the only way in which the heart of the Savior can become our heart.

Through the valleys and deserts, through the hard places of life, we become transformed into His image. As this transformation unfolds, we are freed from looking at life through the old idealistic rose-colored glasses (which always left us in a place of continual disappointment anyway) and we are given the overwhelming privilege of being able to see life through our Savior's eyes.

From this point on, our words are not empty but full of life. Where there used to be vain theory or meaningless platitudes, there is now substance and truth. We no longer live in a world where "ought to" rules our lives. God's Word, purified through our trials, becomes our reality, "a very present help in time of trouble" (Ps. 46:1). Others will sense the life in us and will be transformed by Christ as they hear our words. If God spared us from the pain, He would also be sparing us from the glory.

You may be wondering just how far I'm going to take this. Well, let's return to Paul's words in 2 Corinthians. How far did Paul take the truth of the wounded healer? How deep did his trial get before he entered into resurrection life? He said: "We do not want you to be unaware, brethren, of our affliction which came to us in Asia, that we were burdened excessively beyond our strength so that we despaired even of life" (1:8).

How low did Paul get? How long did God allow suffering to buffet his body, soul, and spirit? If you believe
what Paul wrote here, his trial worked on him to the point
where he was not only beyond his strength, but where he
actually despaired of life. Paul had become so depressed
that he wanted to die. This wasn't some loving wish to be
with the Lord, either. No, Paul really wanted to die. He felt
as if he couldn't take it any longer.

Have you ever felt this way? Don't whip yourself with
guilt. Even the beloved apostle Paul was there.

What did God do when confronted with Paul's depression and despair? Did He fall off His throne when He saw
Paul putting this verse into 2 Corinthians? Did God say,
"Shame on you, Paul. And you call yourself a *Christian*?"
No, our Lord chose to use this trial to help His dear child
increase in the experiential knowledge of His compassion,
deliverance, and complete love. God, in His gracious love,
used this experience to touch Paul with mercy and make
him an even better minister of the gospel.

I believe our Lord's heart broke for Paul. God certainly
saw Paul's depression, but He wasn't disappointed in Paul.
He loved Paul. God reached out to Paul; and as Paul took
God's hand, he was once again given a new depth of understanding toward those he was sent to minister to. God ministered to Paul in a way that not only lifted Paul out of his
depression, but also gave him a new and deeper compassion for others in their own times of depression and despair.

The self-righteous person, the one with no experience
under his belt, would say to Paul, "Now wait a second,
brother! You yourself wrote that God would not give you
more than you could bear. It's right there in your first letter to the Corinthians, chapter 10. You wrote it, Paul! Why
aren't you confessing what you yourself wrote? I don't
want to hear any more talk about despairing of life from
you, brother. That's a negative confession and a pretty poor
testimony to boot!"

Yes, the self-righteous individual will never be able to make any sense at all out of Paul's honest confession. He will either have to ignore its existence in the Bible or simply explain it away ("In the Greek it really means something else, brother").

However, just wait a few years. If you are dedicated to an ongoing walk of faith in the Lord, the time will surely come in your life when you will go through deep and dark trials. You may be desperately clinging to the promises of God and confessing all your favorite Bible verses and it will appear as if God isn't one bit interested in living up to His word to you. It will seem as if He couldn't care less about what you're claiming in His name. You will face such times.

Does this mean God is cruel? Does God, in fact, ignore His promises to us? No, God is not cruel. Nor is He ignoring us or His word. But we cannot use God like some servant whom we command to deliver us when the going gets rough.

We have to come to the place in our life where we say, "Lord this is Your show. I'm no longer going to tell You what to do or how to do it. Have Your way. Even if You don't want to honor Your word to me, that's okay. I know You love me and will never leave me or forsake me. Even though it looks like You've really deserted me this time and Your word seems to be absolutely meaningless, I'm trusting You anyway. I'm choosing to walk by faith and not by sight."

Learning this lesson is not easy. Our faith in God needs to reach the point where we stop trying to figure everything out and stop manipulating God by picking whatever promise we choose. This is the step of faith that frees us from a childish and self-serving interpretation of the Bible. Another way of saying this would be: Real faith is letting go of *our* faith and trusting fully in *His* faith.

When we reach this point in our relationship with God, we are free from the tendency and the need to be self-righteous. The stuffing will have been sufficiently knocked out of us so that from now on, we will walk more humbly and lovingly in His Spirit. We cease making doctrine our God as we finally begin to see Him as He really is. From now on, we will simply want to minister to people out of what God has ministered to us. We will have learned how useless and harmful the typical formulas are, and we will also have learned how all-important God's mercy and compassion are. Out of our darkness we will have indeed discovered a great light.

This is real faith—not bypassing our afflictions or denying their existence, but embracing them in the name and Spirit of Jesus Christ. Choosing to behold His love manifest in us in the midst of our suffering—this is the faith that overcomes the world.

9

Birth of a
Wounded Healer

*N*either George nor Christine Atwell were sighted, but that didn't keep them from boarding a bus in Atlantic City, New Jersey, and traveling way up north to a retreat I was holding in the White Mountains of New Hampshire in November of 1982. Although this was the first time I had met George face-to-face, I felt as if I had already come to know this remarkable person.

George was a regular caller to my "Let's Talk About Jesus" radio program. Whenever he was on the air, I'd keep him on the line for as long as I could. George always ministered to the listening audience. Within a few days of one of his calls, I would begin receiving letters from people who had been encouraged and blessed by the things George had shared.

At my retreat, everybody was talking about George. Whoever met him came away blessed by this brother. What impressed people most about George was his positive, out-going, and loving attitude. George was not going to let anything slow him down; and Lord knows, life had thrown enough at him to slow him down, if not stop him alto-gether. Losing his sight was just one of the many trials George had endured since becoming a Christian.

Before their marriage, Christine had been George's braille teacher. Telling me of their meeting, George said, with a gentle thankfulness in his voice, "I prayed that someone would accept me as I am. My wife does."

George had endured numerous medical crises over the years. But these were not nearly as painful to him as the condemnation he received from fellow Christians for not being completely healed. It was difficult enough trying to cope with a body that was weak and failing, but to have Christian friends reject him for not having a perfectly healthy body—well, that was pretty hard for George to take.

Whenever George called my program, though, his heart of compassion and encouragement always outshone his trials. He only spoke of his hardships in order to uplift some listener who might be suffering too.

George knew what it was like to be afflicted and rejected at the same time, so when he spoke, his words had the ring of reality to them. And George always spoke the truth in love. George "had been there" and had discovered the way out. Love, acceptance, and forgiveness were the avenues to his personal wholeness.

Things hadn't always been this way. When George first called me, he was in the midst of great pain, questioning just about everything he had ever believed. But even in the midst of his suffering and spiritual anguish, George loved God and chose to believe the best about God and about his fellow Christians.

It was a pain-filled path George Atwell walked as he was transformed by God, and by his own willing heart, into a beautiful and Christ-like wounded healer.

I've saved the tapes of conversations George and I had on my radio show. There are three in particular that I'd like to share with you. Each represents a stage George passed through as he struggled to understand the trials he was suffering. These conversations reveal, in a very special and personal way, the process of spiritual evolution one goes through, or grows through, on the path of becoming a wounded healer.

In this first call, we see someone who is in the midst of tremendous anguish, crying out to God and seeking understanding.

George: The reason I am calling is, I have just gotten to the point where it is very hard for me to even pick up the Bible. I've seen now, after ten years of believing and practicing "the faith message," that it doesn't work. And I did everything I was told to do. I maintained every confession. I've literally laughed in the face of death. I've almost died ten times. I've lost my sight. I've had a kidney transplant. I've spent two years on dialysis. I've had a heart attack. I've had all kinds of operations.

The ironic part in all this is that about nine years ago I could see. I had my eyesight.

Because I have diabetes, the doctors told me to keep a real close check on my eyes. Another doctor told me I should have laser surgery done.

But, being a good "faither," I just kept confessing the Word, believing I was healed, because I didn't feel any pain or anything. So . . . I lost my sight.

Another time I had a splinter under my fingernail that you could just barely see. I didn't know it was there because I can't see. I asked people if they could find anything, but they didn't see it either.

Finally, after my finger had bothered me for about three days, I went to the hospital where I found out my finger was infected. I was told that in a couple of days I could have lost my finger.

If I had gone by "the word," confessing my healing, and not by what I feel, I wouldn't have gone to the hospital. And you know, I probably would have lost my finger.

I went to Oklahoma to attend a prayer and healing school. The plan was to stay out there until I had received "my manifestation," you know, my complete healing.

Well, in no time my blood sugar went to way over eleven hundred, which is really, really bad (because, of course, according to this school, if I really believed in my healing, I couldn't keep taking my medication) and I came home three weeks later with kidney failure. Even so, I was going to stay there. I had been conditioned to believe, no matter what the circumstances. But, the doctors gave me two months to live if I did stay there, so I came home.

Wayne: Why did the doctors give you two months to live if you stayed there?

George: Well, because if I stayed there, I wouldn't have been going on dialysis. The doctors told me to get home and get on dialysis. If I hadn't gone home, I probably would have died out there. So I came home, and the doctors were right.

Wayne: What was the advice you received from your Christian brothers and sisters at that time?

George: Well, I didn't listen to a whole lot of what they said at that time. I listened to my parents, and they told me to come home. But some people told me I should have hung in there a little longer and God would have healed me.

I went round and round with this stuff for a long time. It's to the point today that, even talking about it . . . Most times I just feel a lot of guilt. I feel guilt all the time.

Wayne: Why guilt?

George: Well, because I've been made to feel that I did something wrong that put me in this situation that I'm in. I know that . . . that it's really not true.

I know these are, more or less, the cards life has dealt me. I'm diabetic and juvenile diabetics usually have the types of problems that I have. Some of my friends, who have had the same kind of problems I have, are now dead. So I'm very fortunate even to be alive.

I do know that it is not my fault. But being barraged by the faith teaching, day and night for years . . . Now I find it very hard to read the Bible and I haven't listened to Bible tapes for months. The reason is because, and this is maybe not a good reason, probably not, but when I hear any particular Scripture, I can't even look at it without interpreting it the way I had been taught to over the past ten years. It's like I've been brainwashed . . . It's very hard.

I went back to this church I used to attend when I visited my parents. I went there last week and I heard the prayers and a two-hour "confession" presentation.

After the service I was talking to a guy who's been into it for about a year. He was telling me I didn't know what I was talking about, and I've been into it for ten years. I was telling him that the name-it-and-claim-it message works fine for your normal little everyday problems. But the people I'm dealing with . . . like my cousin, who was just put on kidney dialysis last week. He's blind, has diabetes, and his second wife was just killed in a car accident six weeks after their baby was born. And this is the second wife he has lost in an accident. I've got another friend down here at the shore. He's got kidney failure and he has thrown up every day now for six months. He has lost his sight. He is only twenty-four years old, and he is a Christian. So I said to this guy, "What answers do I give these people?"

I mean, I've tried this confession stuff and it didn't work for me. Of course, when I say that to them, they just shake their heads and say I'm full of doubt. They tell me Satan's got a hold of me, that I'm giving up, and all this kind of garbage.

Wayne: So, what did this man say in response to your question?

George: Well, he couldn't answer that. They don't have any answers for this kind of stuff.

There was a guy who was an evangelist, and he was in town about four months ago. He was here for three weeks. He had words of knowledge and was laying hands on people. I tried to pin him down for an answer too. I said, "You know, I've done everything you guys have said to do for years. How come it doesn't work?" He couldn't give me an answer.

I guess . . . well, right now, I haven't lost my faith in God. I love God. I still believe in God, and I've gotten into a group of people who don't believe this way. They are my friends. They're like family to me, and I thank God for that because when I went to the faith teaching, people wouldn't accept anything I had to say because I wasn't healed.

These people let me explain what it's like. Maybe God is showing me and my wife things of His Spirit that He can't show them because they are sighted. So He is showing us in a different way, and maybe they can learn something from it.

I was never accepted for who I was by these other people. They were always pushing my circumstances off, like all they could talk about was something I didn't have, which was my sight and my health. And until I had that . . . they really couldn't accept anything else I had to say. I went through years of this type of treatment.

Wayne: When a person has been fed bad teaching, it's like eating poison. It works its way into your inner being, and even though you may intellectually reject it, there is still a period of time where the teaching, or poison, affects you (especially if the teaching has a lot of guilt-producing mechanics to it, as the teaching you were under does). When you've been fed this type of stuff over a period of years, that subliminal message of guilt, condemnation, faulting, and scapegoating is going to take a while to get out of your system.

It's like when I counsel with someone who has come to Christ but is having a hard time experiencing the love of God. If their earthly father was unloving and uncaring, many times, without even thinking about it, they automatically project those same harsh qualities onto God the Father.

So we have to go through a time of unlearning the old in order to learn the new. This is no instantaneous, or overnight, transformation. It takes time. It takes a lot of time. Sometimes you just have to keep repeating to yourself, "Jesus loves me, this I know, for the Bible tells me so." In other words, you have to get down to the bare bones basics of what the gospel is all about, which is God's love.

You're in a position now of questioning everything. I'm sure this is painful to go through, but it is important to go through it. When you are on the other side of this, you are going to know what you believe, and you're going to know why you believe it.

When you go through a period of questioning your faith, sometimes you come to the honest conclusion that Jesus didn't give you some of the things you've believed. Jesus didn't lead you into these things. He didn't put these destructive and depersonalizing teachings on you. Others put them on you in the name of Jesus, but it wasn't Jesus who did it. It was people with formulas and regulations, who thought they had a handle on the Word of God. So, now you have the difficult task of sifting out the tares from the wheat, separating that which is not life from that which is life. It's painful and I wish I could do it for you, or someone else could, but no one else can. You have to go through this painful process on your own. But pain is a necessary ingredient in our spiritual evolution.

I read a quote recently that said, "Joy sometimes needs pain to give it birth." That's the way it is. You know, George, I believe God is producing something beautiful in you.

George: You know, what hurts more than anything else, is knowing that people reject you as a person in favor of their teachings. And you see people who you thought were your friends, and they're rejecting and breaking contact with you because you no longer see things eye to eye with them. And it's just . . . you know, it just blows me away. It is just very, very hard for me to accept. I don't like anybody not to like me. I try not to do anything bad to anyone—ever. I've tried to be as non-offensive as I can.

Wayne: When you needed acceptance and understanding, you were judged. Instead of receiving compassion from your brothers and sisters, your worth was evaluated according to a doctrine of healing, and you were condemned for not fitting someone's impersonal (and unbiblical) definition of faith.

George: Well, I've always had a spirit like I felt I've been able to overcome things. Even now I'm contemplating going back to college and I just put an application in for a job.

Wayne: Well, here is the hard, yet beautiful truth of life. We might not want it this way, but this is the way it is. We become the people, the ministers of the Lord that we are, effective and compassionate, the spirit of Christ to the world, through that which we suffer. Through our trials, God produces all kinds of beautiful things in us that we have never seen before and that other people may never see.

There was a woman whose writings I have enjoyed. Her name was Hannah Whitall Smith. She wrote a book called *The Christian's Secret of a Happy Life.* This is a fantastic book about possessing a triumphant attitude in the Lord.

However, I'm currently reading her biography and I'm learning that her life, circumstantially speaking, was a nightmare. Four of her seven children died of different diseases. Her husband, who was a famous minister, was involved in a highly publicized affair. A never-ending stream of terrible tragedies came upon her.

Yet it was through these very experiences that Hannah Whitall Smith was given the compassion, grace, and ministry to be such a tremendous source of life and blessing to others.

You said earlier you felt, at one time, that God had called you to the ministry. Perhaps you look at yourself, circumstantially, and say, "Man, I'm a mess. I'm a real mess." But I look at it this way. I believe the most valuable vessels the Lord ever created are the ones who go through much suffering. I'm not saying this is what we want to hear, but this is what is.

God comforts us in all of our afflictions, and by doing so He enables us to comfort people in their afflictions. And you know what? The church is filled with hurting people. The church is overflowing with Christians who love God and yet have been fed so much harmful and destructive teaching. They are hurting and crying out for help.

I believe the people who are going to rise up and be the healers to the church are the ones who are going through their own suffering and are willing to hear the voice of God comforting them. They are learning that there is life on the other side of the cross. When they are raised up, they are going to have life to give to others.

I have every confidence God is going to bring you through this time of hardship, George. He is producing life in you, and not just for yourself. There is a saying that goes, "God doesn't comfort us to make us comfortable, but to make us comforters," and I believe that's what's happening to you.

George: Thank you, Wayne, for this ministry.

Wayne: Be encouraged. God always knows what He is doing, and He is doing something beautiful in you.

In this next conversation, which took place about one year later, we see that the hurt and bitterness George had been suffering through was being replaced with a greater understanding of mercy and forgiveness. Most of all, we can sense the acceptance and love George was experiencing in his relationship with God.

This deepening awareness of God's loving presence in his life was freeing George from the guilt and bondage others had put him under, in the name of God. George is now speaking as a wounded healer.

George: There was a lady who was a friend of mine. And it's kind of strange, because I do understand her mentality. It's coming from the teaching she's getting. She hasn't lived through a situation like my wife and I have. Anyway, she was telling me what a bad testimony I was because I am sick.

Wayne: I think there is only one person you are a poor testimony to, and that's her.

You're not a poor testimony to the world. The world is not going to look at you and say, "Well, he's a Christian and he's blind, so that must mean God's not real." Nobody's going to think that. The sad thing is that no one else is going to think that except her.

I have learned that what really makes a positive impression on those who do not know the Lord are people who know how to love God. Not a superficial love that depends on a Disneyland type of trouble-free existence, but a real "I love God in the midst of my problems" type of love. Many times the person who is the greatest testimony is the one people look at and say, "Man, you've got this problem? How can you love God?" And when that person can say, "Well, listen, God didn't make me blind, you know. I'm not blaming him. He is giving me life. I can see, you know. I see Him. I see His love for me, and I feel His love for you." This is the testimony that I have found the world responds to.

So, to this woman, you're not a good testimony. And as far as I'm concerned, that's *her* problem. If I had witnessed the conversation you had with her, I would have come away thinking that she was the one who was the poor testimony. This intolerance, this judgmentalness, this inability to let common compassion and love overrule pet doctrines, these are the attitudes that turn people off to Christianity.

You won't ever turn the world off by being blind, but this woman's attitude will turn the world off every single time. People see this kind of stuff happening and they say, "Yeah, that's Christianity all right." They see through it right away.

If we're talking about real healing, let's look at the whole picture. True healing doesn't just deal with the body at the expense of hurting the spirit.

People can be so caught up with healing the body that they may become completely insensitive to an individual's spirit and emotions. It's as if they couldn't care less if you leave their service filled with guilt. These types of healing messages mean well, I suppose, but because they are focused only on the body, they can and do inflict real damage on those who are not healed. People who are not healed leave those meetings in worse shape than when they came in.

Someone who is truly acquainted with the healing power of God is going to be continually aware of being good for the individual's body, soul, and spirit. If a minister knows that, then he will always minister in the right spirit.

George: Yeah. One of the things that has always totally puzzled me, and I don't mean to put anybody down when I say this, is that I see certain media ministries on television and I wonder at times why it's always the people who have been healed that they have on their program. There are people who need encouragement, who are going through something like I am right now, who are sick but who are holding on, trusting God, and growing in Him through their affliction. I think about people like this and wonder how come these media ministries never have anything like that on their shows?

I mean, like my cousin, who lost his wife in a car accident, and has all kinds of physical problems. That guy has been through it. But, he still loves the Lord. He's entered a counseling program, and he's now helping other people who have suffered so much. He's growing through his pain, getting on the other side of it, and he's still loving and serving God. Isn't that worth talking about on television?

I think once in a while there ought to be some balance to the healing testimonies, you know, a little bit more to the other side. Not that God wants you to suffer or stay under His thumb. And not that He's gloating over how people are suffering. But a person who still loves the Lord, like my cousin, after all he's been through, I think that's worth something.

Wayne: I agree with you. God can be glorified through someone being healed. But God is also glorified, beautifully, through someone who has had an affliction for a long time, has been in prayer continually, and hasn't been healed. I believe this person has a testimony to share. Loving God and believing in His love, in the midst of affliction, is a message all of us need to hear.

A person like your cousin, and like yourself . . . your life experiences are just as valid and important to the Body of Christ as the person who has been healed.

George: I've been a Christian for fourteen years and I've been through a lot. But there are certain people who won't hear what I say, because . . . well, they say, "What do you know, brother? After all, you're still blind."

Wayne: Right. It's like having a scarlet letter. I think it's so unfortunate that people close their hearts against you. I believe they have a problem that is a far worse handicap than your blindness. That's the truth. They are spiritually blind . . . and they don't know it.

Have you ever met believers who initially really took to you? They may have been attracted to you and had a sincere desire to share the Lord with you, but after a while you feel like they were only willing to give you a certain amount of time. They were willing to have you be one of their causes, but when you didn't roll over and perform as expected (when you didn't get healed), then all of a sudden the warmth, openness, and love turns into criticism and accusation. And eventually they hit the road.

George: Yeah, but it hasn't happened in quite a while. Right now the people around me are attracted to my wife and me because, they say, we have an insight into the Lord that they don't have. They understand, because they are sighted, while we are not, that God deals with us differently. It is like the Scripture in Isaiah 42:16, "I will lead the blind by a way they do not know, in paths they do not know I will guide them. I will make darkness into light before them and rugged places into plains. These are the things I will do, and I will not leave them undone." They look at us as having a different perspective. It's like a guy I heard say one day that the word *disabled* really means "differently abled."

I went to a fellowship a few years back, when I had lost my sight. This was a high-pressure Pentecostal type church. They were telling me I was rebellious, that I was running from God, and this was the reason why I was sick. And man, I knew in my heart I was doing everything in my power to love God and to serve Him. It was a constant condemnation trip.

I shared some of my burdens with the pastor. Shortly after that, one Sunday morning when I was sitting in the service, the pastor looked at me and said when I straightened out my act, when I flew right, wasn't so rebellious (I just didn't agree with him and so I was rebellious in his eyes), he told me that I'd be like this other brother over here who was blind, and that I would be healed.

Well, that other brother is still blind. To this day he is still blind, and this was . . . seven or eight years ago.

It's like the carrot on the end of the stick. This holiness-righteousness thing that you are trying to obtain is the carrot. In their thinking if you reach the carrot you'll get your healing. But no matter how far you walk, the carrot stays on the end of the stick, always just out of reach.

I've found out, through your program, that I am the righteousness of God. I am righteous in Christ already. All of these things are already in me, because He is in me, and He is my righteousness. I may not walk in this awareness every day yet, but I'm learning. I'm learning who I am, and it is not something that . . . Holiness is not something you earn or work for or anything like that. It is just to love God, and to know Him from your heart. I've known Him from my heart for fourteen years, but I just didn't understand because of a lot of teaching I was into.

The people we fellowship with now treat us like we're normal, and this is all we've ever wanted.

I have artificial eyes. Another healing-minister told me to take my eye out and walk around with it out until God healed it.

But these people accept us for who we are, just plain and simple. And when they come over, they are not sticking their thumbs in our eyes, or laying hands on us and shouting in tongues over us, and doing all of this kind of stuff.

A lot of the time the fact that we are handicapped isn't even brought up because we are accepted. That's all we want. We just want to be accepted, you know, and we've found it here.

The last time George Atwell called me on the radio was February 18, 1986. In our final conversation, George's peaceful triumph in Christ was evident as he spoke. This was a time of looking back, summing up, covering the past with mercy and understanding, and giving loving encouragement to those who were struggling with trying to understand their own afflictions.

By God's loving grace, and through his own tender and yielded spirit, George, at last, stood on the mountaintop with a healed heart. He was now able to view his life from the pinnacle of God's everlasting love.

George: One of the things that used to be in the back of my mind was this: If it's God's will for me to be healed, and if I am not healed, then I am not in God's will. Through my whole Christian experience, I always had this cloud hanging over my head—thinking I wasn't in God's will because I was not healed.

Wayne: So, instead of God's healing being a message of hope, it was a guilt trip and type of bondage for you.

George: Right. And even over the last two years, up until this past summer, I was . . . well, for the past two years I had been really bitter. If I even heard the word "faith" coming out of a guy's mouth on the radio, I'd turn it off and get real angry. I felt like that Scripture in Proverbs that says, "Hope deferred maketh the heart sick" (13:12 KJV). That had become true in my life.

I understood, at least partially, what God had done for me. I was beginning to see how much He loves me and who He has made me to be. By knowing this, I began to believe that He has always had my best in His mind. I now know that whatever I go through, He will be there with me, because He loves me.

So, it just stopped being an issue. Now I understand. So many times people pray for things that they already have. They pray to become righteous, when they have already been made righteous through Jesus. Or they pray to become holy, when God has already set them apart for Himself. He has made them holy. People just don't realize . . . I didn't realize, you know. But I'm starting to now. So, that's what I wanted to share.

Wayne: Our walk with the Lord is, in part, a matter of balancing ourselves.

I look at our lives as being like a wheel. Jesus Christ is the hub, or center, of the wheel. There are different spokes going out from the hub. One of the spokes is faith. One of the spokes is grace and another one is works. One of the spokes is listening to the Spirit and another is listening to God's Word. One spoke is loving God and another one is loving man. It's up to us to put these spokes together in such a way that they create a sensibly balanced and effective life.

However, we seem to have the habit of grabbing one spoke and making it out to be the beginning and the end. But a spoke cannot be the beginning and the end. Jesus is the Beginning and the End. He is the hub. He is the one who holds us together. If all our spokes have Him as their meeting ground, then the wheel of our life turns very nicely.

George: I'm beginning to see the Bible as a whole new book. It's a whole different thing now.

For years I couldn't read the Bible without thinking of it in the way I had been told. The faith-teachers had taught me to read things a certain way, so I couldn't see the Scriptures for what they really were. I was reading things into them and seeing verses the way I had been conditioned to see them. And so, for a long time, I wouldn't read it.

I know now that I'm accepted by God for who I am, and not for my works. So, although it's good to read the Word every day, just knowing that I'm accepted helps me so much as I wade through all of my issues. I've still got a lot of things to work my way through, but God has renewed my hope. I am going to get through all this and He is going to be right there with me through it all. He is not going to leave my side. And I now know He never did. He has brought me this far and He is going to keep doing it. He is the author and finisher of my faith. He is going to help me through it all.

But I just want to encourage anybody who is listening, who is handicapped or is going through the same things that I have. Sometimes people put trips on you when they really don't mean to. They don't understand the shape you're in. Whether they haven't taken the time to understand, I don't know. There are probably a million stories similar to mine out there.

Be encouraged. God is not laying a trip on you. He loves you!

One of the things I have learned is that, in the Old Testament law, your acceptance to God was based upon your obedience and your works. But, under the new covenant of grace in Jesus Christ, you can work and be obedient *because* you are accepted. Acceptance comes first and then obedience follows, because of love . . . because of His love.

A few months after our conversation, George went home to be with his Lord Jesus, whom he loved so much.

I miss George. I miss his phone calls and the way he always brought light and encouragement to others during our times of sharing.

Through his many trials, afflictions, and encounters with those who simply refused to see beyond his body into his heart, George Atwell became one of the finest wounded healers I have met. Just like Jesus, George Atwell "learned obedience through the things which He suffered" (Heb. 5:8). George also learned compassion, mercy, understanding, forgiveness, acceptance, and love through the things he suffered.

George is living in perfect acceptance now. I'm sure he's enjoying his new resurrection body, free from all sorrow and blemish. God has wiped away the tears from George's eyes. And now, with new eyes, George at last can see *everything* in God's perfect and glorious light.

I will lead the blind by a way they do not know,
In paths they do not know I will guide them.
I will make darkness into light before them
And rugged places into plains.
These are the things I will do,
And I will not leave them undone.

Isaiah 42:16

10

$\mathcal{L}$iving beyond $\mathcal{J}$udgment

$\mathcal{I}$t's hard to keep your eyes on the light when people always point out the dark places they see in your life.

Maybe your only crime is that you're different. Or perhaps there has been some failure in your life that people, through their judgment, just won't let you forget. Regardless of whether you are "guilty" or not, there comes a time, if you are going to continue living, when you must either sink under or rise above what others think of you. We need to be careful about this, for our self-image can be shaped by the attitudes, opinions, and judgments of others.

Can you see ultraviolet light? No. Even though this light exists, you can't see it with the naked eye. Ultraviolet light is real, but your vision is limited.

That's what being judged is like. People think they see the whole picture of your life, but because their vision is limited, they're really just seeing a piece of it. They don't know that their vision is limited, so they assume that they see all there is to see. Maybe all they see is that you're different, or perhaps they see only your failure, supposed or real. What can you do?

What I encourage you to do is to allow even this to "work together for good." If others have made up their minds about you, you can either choose to live in bondage to their opinion (by believing or trying to change the opinion) or you can release yourself from their opinion. After all, if people have made up their minds about you, aren't you free from trying to impress them?

Even though Paul founded the church at Corinth, he wound up on the receiving end of judgment from his own children in the faith. In his first letter to them, he wrote, "To me it is a very small thing that I should be examined by you, or by any human court; in fact, I do not even examine myself" (4:3). Now here's a man who had discovered his true identity and was not about to accept a definition of himself from someone else. And that's just what judgment is—someone else's definition of you.

Let living under the judgment of others be used of God to draw you to himself. Accept that others judge you, but don't accept their definition of you. Turn the other cheek, but realize their narrow vision is *their* problem. Don't react with anger at the judgment (which is another way of being in bondage to it). Instead, simply understand how limited and insecure we all are. In the same way that Jesus was "despised and rejected" (Isa. 53:3), humbly accept others' rejection and let it make you a better wounded healer. One light-hearted axiom I have learned in life is this: No matter how nice a person you are, somebody thinks you're a jerk.

Let me tell you about one man who learned to live beyond the judgment of others.

"Crazy"—that's what they called Father Gregor Mendel. Even though he is regarded today as the father of modern genetics, in his day Gregor Mendel was considered a quack and a charlatan.

Born in 1822 in Heinzendorf, Austria, Gregor Mendel developed a love for botany early in life, growing up on his father's farm. He entered the Augustinian monastery in 1843 and, except for brief periods of study and teaching, remained in the monastery for the rest of his life.

But Mendel never lost his love for botany.

Through the years he conducted more than thirteen thousand individual case studies involving peas. Mendel's studies proved there were patterns concerning the way characteristics are inherited. Through his laborious studies he discovered it was possible to produce peas showing only recessive characteristics while others showed only dominant characteristics. Mendel was way ahead of his time. This humble monk was seeing things science had yet to discover.

Unfortunately, whenever Gregor Mendel attempted to present his findings to the scientific community of his day, he was only met with ridicule. The experts were so sure they knew the truth concerning genetic research that they vehemently persecuted anyone who challenged their assumption, particularly this "self-made scientist," Father Mendel. All of society was laughing at Gregor Mendel and his wacky study of peas.

When Father Mendel died in 1883, he went to his grave knowing he had made a tremendous breakthrough in the field of genetic research. Yet he also knew his entire life's work had been completely rejected. He died thinking he had failed in his efforts to share his findings and years of research with the world.

To complete this picture of apparent failure, the priest who assumed Father Mendel's post after his death had all his papers burned. All of Mendel's case studies, each painstakingly detailed note, every one of his research papers—all were thrown into the fire. At that time, as far as the church was concerned, Father Mendel was an embarrassment.

Jump ahead seven years. The year is 1900 and the scientific community is buzzing with news of a revolutionary breakthrough in the field of genetic research. Guess what this new breakthrough was. That's right, it was exactly what Father Gregor Mendel had said all along. History was quickly rewritten and Father Gregor Mendel was hailed as the father of modern genetics.

Mendel had been right about his findings, but he never received accolades from his peers during his own lifetime. Even though he lived under the judgment of the whole of contemporary society, he didn't let that dissuade him one bit from being true to himself.

Life can be fickle. One moment you can be a hero, and the next moment you can be a villain. It's all a matter of people's impressions. The wise person is moved by neither the praise nor condemnation of others, but is content to be who he or she is.

Jesus said, concerning the religious establishment of His day, that they loved to kill the prophets, only to turn around and venerate them (Matt. 23:29–31; Luke 13:34).

It's a funny thing about our human nature—we feel threatened by whatever we can't understand. And whatever threatens us we want to silence, because we don't want our neatly defined universe challenged. We don't like to be confronted with truth that forces us to look beyond our accepted boundaries. But life is a constant series of challenges. Doesn't life constantly confront us with new information? When you think about it, isn't life itself constant change?

This is the way of spiritual life. We so often take what we have learned or experienced and treat it as if it were the whole and only truth. We assume, because we love God and are dedicated to the truth, that what we know is all there is to know. In this mindset how can we ever grow in the knowledge of God? How can He reveal something new of Himself to us? If we have all of our beliefs lined up in a row, thinking we have the answer for every question, then haven't we actually limited our field of vision?

This reminds me of the story about the three blind men feeling an elephant. One man, holding the trunk, said, "An elephant is a long snake-like creature." Another man, feeling an ear, thoughtfully said, "No, an elephant is a fairly thin and flat animal." The third man, trying his best to wrap his arms around a leg, rebuked them saying, "You're both crazy. An elephant is extremely large and round." Each man was right, but what they all failed to recognize was that while each had a piece of the truth, no man had the whole truth.

Because his truth didn't fit in with the accepted truth of the day, Father Mendel suffered much in his life. He was a truly good man, yet he was regarded by society as a madman. But the beauty of Gregor Mendel is that he didn't bow under the opinions of others. He simply and humbly continued following God's leading in his life.

What happens to us? Anyone who has a heart for God and who is truly committed to walking in the Spirit is going to go through times of darkness. We will be misunderstood and judged. This is the price we pay as we seek after the approval of God and an unfolding revelation of His truth.

God takes these times of judgment and ridicule and weaves them into His plan for our lives. I believe He allows us to be misunderstood because he knows these experiences will become an integral part of the development of our faith in Him. Will we curse the darkness, defend ourselves, lash back at those who attack us? Or will we entrust our souls to God, humbly living with the judgment of others on us?

In the dark times of life we struggle, wanting to see God at work. The darkness becomes more acute when we are surrounded by people who can only look at our darkness and point a finger. "Hey, brother! Did you know that you're surrounded by darkness?" Thank you very much for that revolutionary insight, but would you care to lend a hand? "Oh, no. I just want to judge you for your darkness. I just want to let you know that you're in darkness." The last thing we need during our dark times is to be surrounded by the "Greek chorus" of people who only condemn us for being in darkness. But that's the way life often is.

In our times of darkness we are given the opportunity to be true to God and to ourselves. When we're all alone, cut off from the approval of our peers, we are actually in a place to hear that "still small voice" of God speaking to us, giving comfort and direction for our lives.

As I indicated earlier, there's a certain freedom you're given when you are living under the judgment of others. After all, if people have made up their minds about you and refuse to change, aren't you, at that point, released from trying to live up to their expectations or gain their approval? Doesn't the judgment of others, as hard as it may be to experience, actually set you free to fix the eye of your spirit completely upon God? So, isn't this ultimately a good thing for your own emotional and spiritual development? Isn't this the path all the prophets and the Son of God walked in their own lifetime?

Others may be convinced that it would be impossible for you to hear from God. After all, in their minds you are in darkness. If you were really loving God, you wouldn't be in darkness, right? Isn't this the conclusion many make? The good person always does right and is blessed as a result—isn't that what many believe? The prevalent, one-dimensional attitude seems to be that if you are really walking in the Lord, you will never be misunderstood, you'll never fall down, be in the wilderness, or endure periods of darkness.

Well, if all this is true, then what does this word from Proverbs mean: "A righteous man falls seven times and rises again" (24:16)? How about that? Don't we think a truly righteous person never falls? We assume if you've fallen, it must mean you can't be righteous because if you were righteous, you wouldn't fall. Do you see the impossible situation created by this thinking? In this mindset, God isn't allowed to use failure in our lives to bring about a greater good. By assuming that the righteous person never falls, we write off anyone in darkness or difficulty. Yet I'm convinced our most important breakthroughs in life may occur during these periods of darkness.

I think the meaning of this verse from Proverbs is that God is not looking at our falls—He's looking at our rising back up. We gain something through our failures.

I remember watching a television show once where innovative and successful business people were being profiled. When asked what they attributed their success to, each one responded, "failure." Not just failure, but getting up from failure and trying again. These folks shared that they felt the only difference between them and unsuccessful people was that they kept getting up. Others may fail and give up, but these folks failed and *got up*. They let their failure bring them to their next attempt.

Watching this program, I was a little surprised at first as I heard these highly successful entrepreneurs talk about how important failure was to their success. But the more I thought about it, the more I realized that in our spiritual lives failure can be our friend too, if only we will get up again.

If others try to keep you down, defining you only by your failure, supposed or real, don't listen to them. God isn't so much interested in whether you've failed or not as He is in whether you will get back up and go on.

Who wants to fail? I know I don't. However, some of us are programmed for failure. For many of us, by the time we come to the Lord, we've already had a whole lifetime of negative and destructive experiences that have profoundly shaped the way we think and act. Is God going to write us all off for having had these experiences? Or will He not, in His own compassion and dedication to our spiritual growth, take all of these experiences, good and bad alike, and work them together for a higher good in our lives?

If we judge another person for failing, could this also be part of our own programming? In other words, who has the real problem here, the one being judged or the one doing the judging? Why would we pass judgment on another anyway? Don't we have enough in our own lives to deal with? And if that's so, is it possible that our judgment of another may really be our own way of avoiding our own personal issues?

The truth is, just like these business people I saw on television, sometimes we don't learn to do things right until we've done them wrong. Some may simplistically say, "Just follow the Word of God." Fine. We all want to do that, don't we? But this simple statement does not take into account the often destructive way our past experiences have programmed us.

In my counseling ministry I've spoken with many good and sensitive people who had given up on God altogether. Why? Because their spiritual peers couldn't accept failure. "Oh, you've failed. Well, that proves you didn't love God. If you loved God, you wouldn't have failed."

But Scripture says, "The righteous man falls seven times and rises again." If you've had major failure in your life, or if you suffer under the unjust label of failure, as Father Mendel did, it is important to recognize that God does not measure you by the judgments of others. If you've failed, then get back up. And if you are called a failure, ignore that label and keep marching forward. That's what God is looking for. Will you get up and move on, or are you going to allow others to define your life for you?

There may always be those who, perhaps out of their own insecurity, will judge you all of your life. Even though

Jesus admonished us to forgive not just one time, or even seven times, but seventy times seven, when we become aware of a sin in somebody's life, we relate to that person on the basis of that sin or failure. I liken this to taking a snapshot of someone at his or her lowest moment and then using that snapshot as the sole basis of evaluating that person.

When I read "the righteous man falls seven times and rises again," I look at it as the Spirit of Christ within you bidding you to get up again.

Don't get stuck in the fall. Rise again.

Disregard the judgment of others. Rise again.

Don't listen to the opinions of those who have written you off. Rise again.

Rise again in the righteousness of Christ, who calls you to eat that failure and let it become life to you. Accept your fall and believe against all belief that God intends to work it for good in your life and in the lives of others.

It would be wonderful if folks would applaud when you get back up and say, "Isn't it great that he kept going even after that terrible fall?" Thank God there will be some folks like that (who probably have failed themselves and have realized there's nothing left to do but either give up or get up). Unfortunately though, you have to accept the distinct possibility that no one will applaud when you get back up. You might fall, be judged by the multitudes, and then watch them move blindly on, unconcerned with your comeback. They've already made up their minds about you. They took their snapshot, and in their minds, that's all they need to know.

When we are in this type of situation, struggling under the judgment of others, let's forget what people think and turn our thoughts instead to what God has for us. Oddly enough, when our reputation is being dragged through the mud, that's when we are given the opportunity to receive a new identity.

Genesis 32 tells us about Jacob wrestling through the night with God. As dawn broke the next day, Jacob continued his hand-to-hand match with the Lord. At last the conflict ended and Jacob was given a new name, a new identity. But at the same time, God put his hand in Jacob's (now Israel's) thigh, and for the rest of his life Jacob walked with a limp.

Perhaps there were some who said, "Jacob, if you had enough faith you'd be healed of that limp." Or, "You wouldn't have that limp if you hadn't wrestled with God." But I think Jacob was purposely given that limp to remind him of the time he wrestled with God, and I believe it also reminded him of his dependency on God.

What do you suppose this account is referring to, symbolically speaking? Jacob wrestled with God through the night, and in the morning he received a new name. I believe this is a picture of what happens to us in our own "night" of darkness. We may feel as if we are wrestling with God; but the result of this intense struggle is that we receive a new name, a new identity, and a new understanding in the morning. We come through the darkness a different person. We're not who we used to be. We have a new perspective, and that is a blessing. But we may also have a limp. We have been wounded, but our wound just reminds us of our dependency on God.

There will always be people who will look only at your darkness, but you can move on. They won't be seeing the "Israel" you have become through your struggle. They will still be seeing "Jacob," or who you used to be, and they'll judge you for having a limp. You'll know you're a different person now, but others may not care. So what do you do? Get back up and go straight ahead. Really, isn't this what you must do?

It's troubling, painful, and hurtful when people who think they know you look only at your darkness. All they seem to see is your failure, and that, in their minds, defines who you are.

Don't listen to them. "The righteous man falls seven times and rises again." Perhaps you've fallen ten times, but the point here is the rising again. The Spirit of Jesus Christ is saying, "Rise again!"

People looked at Father Mendel and thought he was a fraud, yet he stayed true to himself. He didn't accept other people's judgment of him. He didn't let their criticism rock his boat or change his opinion of himself. But what if he had been swayed by the attitudes of others toward him? Suppose he had said, "I'm giving up this study of genetics. What's the point? Why should I bother presenting my findings to the community? All they're going to do is judge me, criticize me, condemn me, and laugh at me."

I believe Father Mendel learned how to live beyond the judgment of others. He knew who he was, and he didn't need somebody else to validate his identity. But the point is, it wasn't until he was being judged that he learned to live above judgment.

If you are in a time of darkness, you may be close to the biggest breakthrough of your life. There are those with limited vision who will only judge you for having gotten into the darkness in the first place. Yes, you're in darkness, and perhaps you even created the darkness you're in. It would be senseless to say, "Yes, I'm in darkness, it's my own fault; therefore, you have the right to judge me for the rest of my life." Just because some are stuck on the issue of how you got into darkness, don't let that dissuade you from seeing what God can create in you through your darkness. The issue is not how you got where you are. The issue is where you're willing to let God take you now.

There's a great prophetic word in Matthew's Gospel, originally from the Book of Isaiah, quoted in reference to Jesus' ministry. The Scripture says, "The people who were sitting in darkness saw a great light; and to those who were sitting in the land and shadow of death, upon them a light dawned" (4:16).

What does "sitting in darkness" mean? I believe it means being stuck, with no forward movement. It speaks of reaching a point where all you can do is sit down. You can't go on anymore. You are at the end of your rope. You've given up, and all that's left is for you to sit in darkness.

If you feel people are looking at you sitting in darkness and have written you off, I believe God looks at you sitting in darkness and says, "This person is ready to see a great light."

I'm staring out my window right now. It's a beautiful sunny day, and there's not a cloud in the sky. If I look up into the sky right now, I'm not able to see the stars. Why? Because it's daylight. But tonight, if the cloud cover doesn't roll in, I'll see the stars. Because of the darkness of night, I will be able to see the light of the stars. Similarly, I believe our darkness just makes God's light shine all the brighter.

So it is with all of us. Jesus said those who think they are healthy do not need a physician. He said He came for the sick and not the well. So the people who knew they were sick were able to let Jesus touch them, while those who thought they were well weren't aware of their own inner sickness and need for Jesus' touch in their lives.

Those who think they're fine and look at others as sick are not going to receive any help. Why? Because they don't think they need help, so they're not open to help. But if you're sick and you know you're sick—if you're in darkness and you know you're in darkness—then you are a prime candidate to see a great light and receive a healing touch.

"The people who were sitting in darkness saw a great light; and to those who were sitting in the land and shadow of death, upon them a light dawned." Isaiah didn't say the light dawned upon the righteous. The dawning light was for the people who were sitting in the land and shadow of death.

What is the land and shadow of death? It's the land of complete despair. It's hopelessness. It's the bottom of the barrel and then some. It's when you've exhausted everything you have and you're still coming up short. It's when you're surrounded by people coming at you, in the name of God, pointing a finger at your darkness or defining you in terms of what they think your sins are.

If you feel like you're in a land of great darkness and you're saying, "I just can't take it anymore," I believe, 100 percent, that a light is about to dawn. A great light is ready to appear for you. Forget about the judgment of others, fix your eye completely on the goodness of God, and let Him shine His light on you.

As for Father Gregor Mendel, I'm sure he would have appreciated being recognized for his life's work. But I believe the rejection of others played a part in his determination to continue his genetic studies. In the same way Father Gregor Mendel remained true to himself and to what he believed, enduring the darkness while ignoring the opinions of others, so I encourage you. Don't let the judgment and condemnation of others keep you from seeing the principle that in darkness a great light shines. If you've fallen down, no matter what the reason, I urge you right now to rise again and see yourself as righteous for doing so. Put all the judgment you've received into the hands of God and let Him cause this to work together for good.

When your darkness passes, you will be seeing your true self, your new self in God, more clearly and more compassionately than you ever have before. And you will be able to see all others with that same compassion. For having been in the darkness, you will have a great light and will have become a more able wounded healer to those who sit in their darkness.

11

*A*rise and *E*at

*H*as there ever been a time in your life when things seemed so dark and hopeless that you actually wanted to die? If so, then you're in good company.

Elijah, that great Old Testament prophet, reached a point during his ministry where he prayed for death (1 Kings 19:4). Jonah was another prophet who went through a period of wanting to die (Jonah 4:3). And as we have already seen, Paul experienced a despair so intense that he called out for death (2 Cor. 1:8). This tells me something; you can love God with the best of them and still have a setback in your life so complete that all desire for living can be completely removed from you.

Some say Christians should never feel depressed, but I think that opinion is irrelevant. If you feel so emotionally beat up that you're actually asking for death, it doesn't help to hear someone tell you it's wrong to feel that way.

Actually, the more you are told it's wrong to feel depressed, the worse you'll probably feel. Now, in addition to being in despair, you'll also feel that you're letting down God, your brothers and sisters, and the rest of the universe.

But there is a way out of the pit of despair. Let me tell you the story of how God brought Elijah through his dark night of the soul.

In the eighteenth chapter of 1 Kings, we see Elijah at the most powerful moment of his life. He had just been in a head-to-head confrontation with wicked King Ahab's pagan prophets of Baal. In a contest with Elijah, King Ahab's prophets sang, shouted, danced, and even wounded themselves all day long attempting to coax their god Baal to come forth and consume their sacrifice with fire. Nothing happened.

Then Elijah took his turn. He carefully built his altar, and as an additional act of confidence, he completely drenched it with water. The Lord God of Israel triumphantly came down in a fiery blaze and consumed the entire sacrifice. With emotions running high, the crowd attacked the prophets of Baal, slaying them all. What an incredible day of power Elijah experienced!

King Ahab gave the bad news of their prophets' defeat to his wife, Queen Jezebel, who was even more wicked than he was. Together these two had tried to exterminate all the true prophets of the living God from the land of Israel. In response to this unexpected failure, Jezebel sent the following message to Elijah: "So may the gods do to me and even more if I do not make your life as the life of one of them by tomorrow about this time." In other words, Jezebel was saying, "Elijah, you've got about twenty-four hours to live."

What a startling change of events! In less than a few hours, Elijah's pinnacle of victory had been turned into a sentence of death.

Forget about how life *ought* to be; this is how it really *is*. We can have our best experience ever in God *today*, only to have our worst experience *tomorrow.* I'm glad to know we have a good and powerful God who truly ministers to us in the rough and tumble of life. Whether we're having a great day or a terrible day, He remains the same, consistently giving comfort and strength to us.

Peter is a classic example of how your best day can become your worst in the blink of an eye. Once when Jesus asked His disciples who they thought He was, Peter declared, "Thou art the Christ, the Son of the Living God." Jesus replied, "Blessed are you, Simon Barjona, because flesh and blood did not reveal this to you, but My Father who is in heaven" (Matt. 16:16–17). Now drop down a few lines in your Bible. It's later in the day and Jesus is telling His disciples He's bound for Jerusalem and there He will die. Peter cries out, "God forbid it, Lord! This shall never happen to You." Jesus then declares to "blessed" Peter, "Get behind Me, Satan" (vv. 21–23). In the space of a few lines, Peter went from being praised by Jesus to being rebuked by Jesus for being in league with the devil.

That's the way it happened to Peter, and sometimes that's the way life happens to us. One moment we're on the mountaintop, praising God for all His blessings and thanking Him for His presence. Then, in a flash, life can throw us into a valley so deep that we are completely unable to see any reason to live.

Perhaps we're riding high on a big victory, and we let our guard down. Or maybe we're becoming puffed up, and the blessing we just received needs to be met with a lesson in humility. Whatever the case, sometimes it's the mercy of God that sticks out the almighty foot, sending us sprawling into next week, so we may return once more to walking humbly in the mercy and compassion of Jesus.

So here's Elijah, absolutely thrilled with his fantastic victory over the prophets of Baal, and Jezebel says, "By this time tomorrow you will die." After what Elijah just witnessed, you might think he'd just shake off this threat. Right? Wrong.

Do you recall what James said about Elijah in the fifth chapter of his letter? "Elijah was a man with a nature like ours" (v. 17). In other words, Elijah was a regular guy. He wasn't "Super-saint," always walking three feet off the ground. The sooner we give up this idea of super-saints, the better off we are going to be. Regardless of what we think Elijah should have done, the Scripture says that when he heard Jezebel's vow, "He was afraid and arose and ran for his life" (1 Kings 19:3).

Elijah didn't laugh in the face of death this time. He split. His big victory of faith all but disappeared in the face of Jezebel's proclamation.

Before you judge Elijah, let me ask you: Are your emotions always rational? You know they're not. It's senseless to put ourselves on guilt trips over the way we feel. Beating ourselves up, thinking we should feel a certain way (if we "really" love God)—this never changes anything, except it usually makes us feel worse. The old line of thinking that certain emotions are spiritual while others are carnal is, I believe, ultimately damaging to our sense of worth and value to God. Our emotions sometimes simply take us over. We often don't even know why we feel the way we do.

The only true victory over our emotions is to accept them all, realizing God is looking on our hearts and not merely at our external expressions. He's not expecting us to be some sunshiny-twenty-four-hour-a-day-cheerful-tiptoe-through-the-tulips type of believer. The love of God goes much deeper than that. He sees the root of our emotions with compassion. His Spirit gently ministers to our hearts at our point of need. If anything is going to help our emotional stability, it is this: seeing God loving us for who we are and not only for how we feel.

God is interested in ministering to you right now. That's what He wants. He's not interested in pointing a finger of blame about how you got where you are. And He's certainly not interested in moralizing about "spiritually acceptable" emotions. He desires to give you His life along with the knowledge of His presence because He knows this will truly lift you out of despair. In the final analysis, I believe this is what God cares about most—delivering you from despair and bringing you back into the land of the living. He's not looking so much at the cause of the problem as at the solution, which is His love.

However, Elijah did what we're all good at doing when faced with seemingly insurmountable obstacles—he ran for his life. He took off for Beersheba in the southern wilderness. When he got there, he dumped his servant and then went another day's journey farther into the wilderness. This is someone who really wanted to be alone.

Elijah didn't want anyone to know where he had gone. He didn't even let his servant know. That's how scared he was. He headed straight into the wilderness and hoped that no one, especially Jezebel's soldiers, would be able to find him. He tried to disappear in the seemingly never-ending network of desert mountains and canyons.

When he thought he had run far enough to escape Jezebel's clutches, Elijah finally came to rest under a juniper tree. This was where he prayed to die. Isn't it strange that while on the one hand Elijah runs to save his life, on the other hand, he requests to die? He wanted to live, yet he wanted to die. I think Elijah had reached that point of emotional burnout where he just didn't care anymore. He was on the verge of a breakdown.

Elijah prayed, "It is enough; now, O Lord, take my life, for I am not better than my fathers" (1 Kings 19:4). When you've been mightily used of God, and then within twenty-four hours the whole bottom of your life drops out, that can really set you back. Elijah had very quickly reached that point of despair where no amount of faith or remembrance of past miracles was going to alter the black hole he was staring into.

Completely exhausted and with no remaining hope or desire to live, Elijah "lay down and slept under a juniper tree; and behold, there was an angel touching him, and he said to him, 'Arise, eat'" (v. 5).

"Arise, eat." If life looks as if it's closing in on you, and there's no point in going on any longer, these are the sweetest two words you can hear—"Arise, eat." Maybe you think you've blown it so badly that there's no way things can turn around—"Arise, eat." Perhaps your circumstances can't back up to where they used to be, but God can still take this situation and make it life and sustenance for you—"Arise, eat." God is a God of life, and He's got two words to say to you if you're being overwhelmed with troubles and despair—"Arise, eat."

Perhaps you feel you're in the same sort of spot Elijah was in. If you are, then I believe you are actually in a good place. It was here that the angel of the Lord came and touched Elijah, saying, "Arise, eat." The angel didn't merely tell Elijah what to do. He actually enabled him to do it: "Then he looked and behold, there was at his head a bread cake baked on hot stones, and a jar of water" (v. 6). God didn't just tell Elijah what to do. No. He gave him direction, and then he also gave him what he needed (the food) to follow this life-giving direction.

I hope you'll let God feed you. I'm not talking about the Almighty tossing a couple of burgers on the grill. I'm talking about eating food from God, food from His own heart. Be willing to believe God wants you to live. Believe He has a purpose for you. Believe there is a life of fulfillment for you in Him. This is what the angel meant when he said, "Arise, eat."

Elijah had reached a point where he thought it was all over. He gave up. But when the angel touched him and fed him, this was God's way of encouraging Elijah to hope again. This wasn't one of these I'll-give-it-one-more-shot attempts on Elijah's part. No, God was saying to Elijah, "If you will arise and eat my food, you will gain new strength, purpose, and direction for your life."

Can you hear the gentle voice of God calling you through this message? Can you hear that inner voice from the deepest part of your being saying, "Yes, I will arise and eat. I'll eat God's food, be filled with His strength, and arise to a new day of living—living in the presence of God." Simply begin by drinking in His Spirit, eating from His goodness, from His heart, and from His love.

Your circumstances might not change immediately. Elijah's didn't. The Scripture continues by saying, "So he ate and drank and lay down again" (v. 6). I'm sure Elijah appreciated this heavenly-catered meal, but his exhaustion was so great that he ate the angel's food and then went back to sleep. God wasn't angry with Elijah for going back to sleep. God wasn't up in heaven looking down at Elijah with some set of divine expectations. No, God saw Elijah with mercy and compassion, beholding his needs and meeting them with His own tenderness.

"And the angel of the Lord came again a second time" (v. 7). The first time the angel said, "Arise, eat"—two simple words. However, this first visit from the angel apparently was not enough to get Elijah going. So what did God do? Did he say, "Hey, I gave Elijah a chance and he blew it"? No, of course not. Maybe some people are like that, and maybe some people even think God is like that, but the beauty of this passage is that God kept on giving. Even if we don't have the strength to receive what He is giving, He will make us strong enough so we may receive what He wants to give us. That's what I call commitment.

So God sent His angel again. This time the angel said, "Arise, eat, because the journey is too great for you." What a wonderful word. Elijah was so depressed that he couldn't even figure out why the angel was feeding him. Perhaps all Elijah could see was this one little meal. I think God sent the angel to feed Elijah in order for Elijah to see that by himself he wasn't going to make it. This journey was too great for him. But God was assuring Elijah that he wasn't in this by himself.

All by ourselves, this journey of life is too great for us. But we are not in this by ourselves! This is what we need to see. Sometimes it's not until we're ready to give up that we at last recognize that God has been patiently waiting to show us we are not alone. In our emptiness He touches us with His presence so that we may become aware of His desire to feed and nurture our spirit.

Your life isn't over. Maybe hardships have brought you to a point of despair. If you're willing to let God join you now in your despair, then all of these apparent negative circumstances will have actually brought you to a good place.

You might say, "Oh, but Wayne, you don't know what I've done." You're right. I don't know what you've done. But I do know God. I know God does not show partiality. He loves you with His whole heart. What you've done is not the issue right now. What matters now is seeing what God wants for you. And He wants you to live, not by yourself any longer, but in a dynamic relationship with Him.

God wants you to live. He has a purpose for you. I encourage you to take all the darkness surrounding you and let it serve to bring you to this point where you will let God feed you and cause you to truly live. "Arise and eat." Receiving this word opens the door for you to be aware of being fed from His own hand.

Perhaps you are depressed because you've come face-to-face with aspects of your life that aren't working. If this is the case, then you're actually in a good place, because now you can see what really does work in life. Stand and see the salvation and deliverance of the Lord. You will come through these circumstances a changed person. You will have a greater awareness of your true life being in God, and that makes all the difference.

"So he arose and ate and drank, and he went in the strength of that food forty days and forty nights to Horeb, the mountain of God" (v. 8). In the Scriptures, going to the mountain represents going to God. God fed and strengthened His child so he could go to Him. Elijah was strengthened by God's food so he could go to God's mountain. The beautiful truth in this verse is that even if we feel we don't have the strength left to go to God, He will give us that strength. In other words, God will do anything and everything possible to enable us to go to Him.

Elijah went to the mountain of God. It's one thing to decide to live—that's good. But now, how about a purpose for living? "He came there to a cave, and lodged there; and behold, the word of the LORD came to him, and He said to him, 'What are you doing here, Elijah?'" (v. 9). God challenged Elijah to consider his life's purpose. The Lord enabled Elijah to come to Him, and then he said, "What's the point? What's your purpose, Elijah? Why are you here?" God had brought Elijah to the mountain in order to give him a new perspective and purpose for living.

At this point, Elijah remained stuck in his despair, so he could only answer according to the negative circumstances that had led him there. Even though angels were feeding him and God was talking to him, Elijah still wasn't seeing the positive outworking of these apparently negative circumstances. He said, "I have been very zealous for the LORD, the God of hosts; for the sons of Israel have forsaken Thy covenant, torn down Thine altars and killed Thy prophets with the sword. And I alone am left; and they seek my life, to take it away" (v. 10). Elijah answered God's question in a completely negative way. He still wasn't recognizing God's hand in these events. Elijah thought he was in the wilderness to escape death, but God had brought him there to receive life. There's quite a big difference between these two points of view, isn't there?

I'm thankful that God never takes His eye off His goal for our lives. Rather than being put off by Elijah's gloomy outlook, He replied, "Go forth, and stand on the mountain before the LORD" (v. 11). This is where you and I receive our true purpose, when we are willing to stand on the mountain before the Lord.

As we look at Him, seeking to behold His true nature, we begin to be transformed. Even though our circumstances may not change, *everything* changes because *we* are changing. As long as Elijah was running, he wouldn't be able to see the higher-life perspective in the midst of his troubles. But now that he was alone in the wilderness, standing on the mountain, God had his undivided attention. Elijah was about to receive a divine object lesson concerning God's true nature and purpose.

What is your concept of God? I've counseled with many folks who have such a distorted image of God that, in some cases, it has destroyed their lives. Do you think of God as that wrathful, vengeful judge who's just waiting to club you over the head with his celestial baseball bat the first time you trip up? I've met many people who feel so strongly this way that I think their faith has done them more harm than good.

But I've got a different God than that. My Lord redeems everything. My God makes good come out of even the darkest circumstances (Rom. 8:28). He doesn't lose anything. He never stops loving. Even the hairs of our head are counted. If a small, insignificant sparrow falls to the ground, God knows about it (Matt. 10:29–31). I don't believe this conditional step-out-of-line-and-God-will-have-nothing-to-do-with-you religion is Christianity at all, for it has nothing to do with the person of Jesus Christ.

Before God can truly touch us in the deepest recesses of our being, taking away our fear of life or our depression,

He first needs to change our image of Him. This is what He did for Elijah. Elijah was so wrapped up in the negative that he couldn't see the positive at all. So, instead of giving up on Elijah, God decided to help him by giving him a demonstration that would teach Elijah about His own gentle and compassionate nature.

God said, "'Go forth, and stand on the mountain before the LORD.' And behold, the LORD was passing by! And a great and strong wind was rending the mountains and breaking in pieces the rocks before the LORD; but the LORD was not in the wind" (v. 11). Some people can relate to God only through His awesome power. To these people, God is powerful, but that's all. There's no tenderness or personal care in that mentality.

"And after the wind an earthquake, but the LORD was not in the earthquake" (v. 11). Some people think the Lord is always after them, shaking things up and destroying everything in their lives. That's not God either. Life may do that to us, but God is dedicated to putting us together, not tearing us apart.

"And after the earthquake a fire, but the LORD was not in the fire" (v. 12). Some people think God wants to burn up everything they have. They mistakenly take the concept of an all-powerful God and assume that God will take away from them anything they want. They think they have to do what they don't want to do and they cannot do what they want to do. In the minds of these poor souls, God burns all the good up and just leaves them with one agonizing trial after another. But that is not God either!

"And after the fire a sound of a gentle blowing. And it came about when Elijah heard it, that he wrapped his face in his mantle, and went out and stood in the entrance of the cave" (vv. 12–13). Elijah's mantle represented his faith, or his true spiritual self. In 2 Kings 2 we are told of Elijah's departure into heaven. As he was being taken up in a chariot of fire, he left his mantle behind for his servant Elisha, who had requested a double anointing of Elijah's power. So, when Elijah wrapped his face in his mantle, he was choosing to see his spiritual self. His face was what he saw with; and his mantle was his spiritual identity. When Elijah put his face in his mantle, he finally began seeing the true nature of God.

Elijah left the cave when the gentle wind came by. In other words, it was the gentleness of God that drew Elijah out of his cave.

If you think God is into breaking rocks, shaking the earth, and burning everything up, chances are you'll stay in your own dark cave. But if you are willing to hear the gentle wind of God and to wrap your face in your mantle, then I believe you will be drawn out of your cave of despair into the sunshine of God's divine love, care, and purpose for you.

Many people unknowingly project their own fears and life experiences onto their image of God. But they're not touching the heart of God! It's as if they are standing on the outside looking in. They're like Elijah, hiding in a cave. They may be devout Christians and true Bible believers, but they don't know the essence of God. Instead of being created in the image of God, they have actually dragged God down to their level and have unintentionally made Him in their image. As with Elijah, their wrong concept of God makes them draw wrong conclusions about life.

If you will simply let God speak these words of life to you, "Arise and eat," you will soon see Him ministering to you and giving you a good purpose in life. You, too, can step out of your cave. I encourage you right now to wrap your face in your mantle, see your true identity in Christ, and begin looking with the eyes of faith at God's committed goodness in your life.

After this awesome demonstration from God concerning His true nature, Elijah went out and stood in the entrance of the cave. "And behold a voice came to him and said to him, 'What are you doing here, Elijah?'" (v. 13). God asked Elijah the exact same question He asked before. I think God was showing Elijah, and us, the key to discovering true joy and fulfillment in life. Through this experience I see God tying together a true knowledge of Himself with the realization of our life's purpose. If you know the heart of God, you will be able to sense your true purpose and high calling in life.

Many people don't know the heart of God. This, all by itself, is the grandest purpose—to know God as He really is and to be an expresser of His true nature to this world. I can't think of a higher goal in life than that of living in an intimate relationship with God. Once we see this as our high calling, all of life takes on new meaning and vibrancy.

Have circumstances in your life brought you to the place where you are considering ending it all? I believe that in God's hands, you are potentially at the single greatest turning point of your life. If everything in your experience has brought you to the point of utter despair that you're in today, *even if your circumstances have been of your own creation,* that doesn't matter right now. Perhaps your circumstances have shown you vividly that life, all by itself, leads to one dismal end. If that's the case, good, because now you have a point of comparison. You, perhaps more than others, have the benefit of knowing what life outside of God's goodness can do to you. Now, as the Lord feeds you, you will have a new awakening appreciation of life that maybe you would have never dreamed possible.

What matters right now is letting God speak to you. "Arise, eat, and go to the mountain of God." Stand and see and keep on seeing until you hear the gentle voice of God. Let God correct your image of Himself. Let Him show you His love and compassion. Let Him feed you and sustain you with His own presence. Let Him give you the joy of living in fellowship with Himself. From now on, approach each day as a shining, divine opportunity for you to experience more and more of God's all-encompassing love toward you and in you. If you will simply do this, you will have all the life and purpose you need in order to live in peace, joy, and abundance. This is the absolute highest form of keeping your eyes on the light.

Arise and eat, for you are no longer alone on your journey.

12

The Child Within

*H*e didn't have any clothes on and he didn't care at all. I, along with everyone else, was lying sedately in the sun, quietly enjoying a day at the shore. But this little boy of four or five was completely taken up in the wondrous experience of the beach. It was all new to him and it was all full of life. He'd run up to the waves as if taunting them. And then, when they came in toward him, he'd run away, waving his hands in the air and squealing with delight.

It struck me that all of us "adults" were very reserved while this boy had no reservations. We were all quietly image conscious, positioned in our chairs or hiding in our books, while this child gave way to joy and laughter. What made the difference? We were afraid; he was not. Perhaps other "adults" were watching this boy and wishing they were young again so that they too could let themselves be completely absorbed in the simple joy of being at the beach. But this child was doing it. His nakedness wasn't lewd. It was innocent. It was beautiful. It spoke of a complete rapture in the now with a beautiful ignorance of everything else. We "adults" were mature in our knowledge, but this child was joyful in his innocence.

As I watched this child playing at the beach, it reminded me of my early days as a believer, when everything was full of wonder and excitement.

Did you have a "honeymoon" experience when you first came into an awareness of God's love for you? Was everything sunshine and light during those first golden days of faith?

That's the way it was for me. It was great. Here I was, an undeserving sinner, and I was loved. I felt as if all of my problems had been wiped away and in their place was the beautiful revelation of being a child of God. Nothing could touch me. I was forgiven, redeemed from the empty darkness, and set apart for the Lord of the universe. Back in those early days I was floating on a cloud, high above the world.

It's interesting to note that this blissful feeling occurred in my life when I was a babe in Christ and knew absolutely nothing concerning doctrine or theology. In retrospect I see that, when I began to be preoccupied with "the right way to act" and with all the dos and don'ts, that's when the love began to ebb and guilt began to grow. Sound familiar?

I believe this early sensing of joy has a lot to do with Jesus' statement about our need to become as little children in order to enter the kingdom of God (Matt. 18:30). While some may look at this verse as referring only to one's initial acceptance of Christ, I see the meaning of this Scripture in a broader context. I believe being childlike is a continuing need in our lives. Jesus was saying that only through a childlike trust in His Word (without trying to figure it all out or doctrinalize it into oblivion) can we fully enjoy the blessings of His kingdom in our hearts.

I've been living this Christian life for over twenty years and I still hear God telling me to be like a child. When I listen to Him and practice being a child (yes, I've learned it takes great dedication to be a child before Him), that's when my faith is strongest and I sense His presence most fully.

Some perceive Christianity as a series of stages, or levels, of growth. This idea may come from John's first letter in which he said: "I am writing to you, little children, because your sins are forgiven you for His name's sake. I am writing to you, fathers, because you know Him who has been from the beginning. I am writing to you, young men, because you have overcome the evil one. I have written to you, children, because you know the Father. I have written to you, fathers, because you know Him who has been from the beginning. I have written to you, young men, because you are strong, and the word of God abides in you, and you have overcome the evil one" (1 John 2:12–14).

John addressed three distinct groups of Christians within this passage: children, young men, and fathers. Some believe we are to grow through the "child" stage into the "young man" stage, and when we have "arrived" (meaning when we agree with whatever doctrine we have been taught), we can finally be considered "fathers." According to this line of reasoning, the child is nothing more than the first stage of our Christian experience. I think it is a great error to draw this conclusion.

While these three terms—child, young man, and father—do describe different stages in the Christian life, I see them as being interrelated and interdependent rather than independent of each other.

If we forget what we know as children and instead choose to revel in some kind of ego-satisfying conviction that we are fathers, then we have missed the point. We need to back up and relearn what it means to be a child. To me, a true spiritual father wouldn't even claim such a title for himself. After all, revelation of truth is not simply for our sakes but for others. The father, in his knowledge and wisdom, would realize the essential value of remaining in the simplicity (and humility) of the child and the power of the young man.

So, I don't see child, young man, and father as three separate stages, or classes, of Christianity. I see these classifications as being descriptive of different parts of our awareness of who we are in the family of God. We need to be children all of the time. We need to be young men all of the time. And we need to be fathers all of the time. Obviously, we are children before we are young men and fathers, but it would be a big mistake to leave one stage behind for another.

To simplify, here's the way I describe it:

The child in us receives the truth of God's Word with
    simplicity.
The young man in us stands fast, holding onto the truth.
The father in us possesses the wisdom to understand and
    apply the truth.

When we are in that initial "little child" stage, just like the boy at the beach, the whole world is filled with beauty and wonder. Understandably, we'd like things to remain that way. We want to stay on our mountaintop and we certainly don't want to hear any talk about trials, tribulations, or the dark side of Christianity. We want God to be fully understandable and we want all of our questions answered in a black-and-white, cut-and-dried fashion.

It's natural to want to hold onto a simplified view of the world. I'm not advocating giving that up any sooner than God forces you to. Enjoy and experience the love of God fully during this time because you are going to need the knowledge of that gentle and constant love during the storms of life. Get to know the heart and nature of your gracious Lord as much as you can during your "honeymoon."

The quickest way to fall away from this childlike faith and love is to become sidetracked onto a works-oriented lifestyle where everything depends on your performance. It is unfortunate that many churches emphasize God's love and forgiveness only when preaching to unbelievers. Once the unbeliever becomes a believer, he or she seldom hears of a gracious and merciful God. In His place appears a new god who, apparently, would just as soon judge you as look at you. This is a two-faced god who forgives years of sin in order for you to become his child, then turns completely around and makes remaining his child totally dependent on flawless performance. Somehow, in this theology, you couldn't save yourself, but you are fully expected to keep yourself saved.

Rubbish!

There's no true heart relationship possible in this way of thinking. If, every time you make a mistake, the wrath of God falls on you, then how are you going to grow? By stopping all mistakes? You see, the only way you could truly grow would be to reach that mythical place of sinless perfection, twenty-four hours a day. Since this is impossible, the only other way you could hold onto your sanity in this type of environment would be to deny your own flaws and concentrate on the flaws of others. Either way, you're not going to be able to grow in the grace and knowledge of Jesus Christ (2 Peter 3:18), because you will be forever preoccupied with your own performance. By putting the sole responsibility of your faith on your own shoulders, you will, in effect, be making your Christianity revolve around yourself rather than Jesus Christ. It's no wonder that a person in this type of environment would have no awareness at all concerning God's great love.

John wrote, "We love, because He first loved us" (1 John 4:19). According to this verse, we don't serve in order to prove how worthy we are or how thankful we are. Nor do we serve in order to earn something from God or maintain our position before God. We serve because it is our natural response to the love that has been bestowed upon us. Service, in its purest sense, is nothing more than our response to the grace of God. We serve simply because it is love to serve. In other words, the love God freely bestows upon us is the *generator* of our own love. As I behold His love for me, warts and all, I find myself loving Him more and more.

However, if I am being ordered to love God, out of some mistaken concept that my act of love will make Him love me in return or bless me, then I actually lose sight of His love altogether. As soon as the focus is off Him and on me, not only am I not able to truly love, but I become bogged down, seeing all the ways my love is lacking.

I have counseled many individuals who were thrust into the situation I'm describing ("now that you're saved, here is what you must do"). They have been severely damaged, not only spiritually but emotionally and psychologically as well. It's as if they were torn from their mother at birth, denied that all-important nurturing and bonding period, and were instead thrown into the army. I call this "spiritual child abuse," and it's all too common.

You may be familiar with a poem called "Children Learn What They Live." It contains much wisdom for children, and can easily be applied to what happens to us as children of God.

Children Learn What They Live

> If a child lives with criticism,
> he learns to condemn.
> If a child lives with security,
> he learns to have faith.
>
> If a child lives with hostility,
> he learns to fight.
> If a child lives with fairness,
> he learns justice.

If a child lives with ridicule,
   he learns to be shy.
If a child lives with praise,
   he learns to appreciate.

If a child lives with shame,
   he learns to feel guilty.
If a child lives with encouragement,
   he learns confidence.

If a child lives with tolerance,
   he learns to be patient.
If a child lives with approval,
   he learns to like himself.

If a child lives with acceptance and friendship,
   he learns to find love in the world.

                     Author unknown

As this insight-filled poem so beautifully states, the environment we live in—whether it be home, school, church, or otherwise—plays a major role in our character development. Keeping this in mind, how can a newborn Christian hope to truly know God's love if he or she is, in essence, ripped from the womb, all in the name of being a disciple? Even as people are being told to "live right and be holy," their very critical and judgmental environment insures they will be relating to God more on the basis of shame and guilt than love. All their striving for perfection may actually produce the opposite of what God's love would produce in them.

Doing God's will (always determined by someone else for you) seems to be the one and only issue in this guilt-filled mindset. The idea of growing in the knowledge of God's true loving nature is pretty much ignored. Therefore, in a very real sense, the spiritual child has no parent, no bonding experience, and suffers as a result. Even though this whole approach is, theoretically, supposed to make one a "good Christian," I've come to believe this type of high-pressure environment has little, if anything, to do with Christianity. The word *Christian* literally means "a follower of Jesus Christ." Living in God's love produces a healthy self-image, security, and a sense of peace, enabling an individual to be a true follower of Jesus, simply because the believer is primarily relating to Jesus. However, the spiritual child thrust into a performance-oriented religion is going to wage a life-long battle with guilt and anger. A Christianity not centered on the true nature and finished work of Jesus Christ can only distort everything about God's character, purpose, and love for people.

In his brief epistle, Jude wrote, "Keep yourselves in the love of God" (v. 21). That's a good place to start the Christian life and, I've come to believe, a good place to *keep* your Christian life. When the chips are down, teachings and dogma will fail us every time. All of our efforts and works may amount to nothing when we are in our hour of need. But the love of God will always uphold us and bring us safely through to the other side.

The Bible declares that even our work for God is born out of His love for us. Isn't this what Paul was referring to when he said, "For we are His workmanship, created in Christ Jesus for good works, which God prepared beforehand, that we should walk in them" (Eph. 2:10)? You see, our obedience, or work for God, has never been the issue. The issue is always . . . Him. And Paul tells us that He has even prepared our good works. Now that's love! All we have to do is walk in Christ, resting in His loving presence and Spirit, and we will discover ourselves naturally fulfilling that which He has called us to do.

Our "honeymoon" is precious. We need to be diligent to keep ourselves in the glow of that first love at all times. We must not let circumstances rob us of the knowledge of our Savior's love. That's why the child within us is so important, because this is the part of us that keeps receiving God's unconditional love, simply and in full trust, regardless of all outside influences.

However, the day will arrive when the rug is pulled out from under you and you're left lying flat on your back, wondering where God went. Love seems nowhere to be found. There is just an awful emptiness and silence where there used to be such a sweet communion with the Most High.

When you first encounter this type of experience, you may cry out, "My God, my God, why hast thou forsaken me?" and you may honestly believe this is exactly what He has done. Where has He gone? Why won't He stop the pain? Why are your prayers going unanswered? Why do you feel so alone?

As painful as this experience may be, I believe it is an absolutely necessary part of the process of our growing up into mature, fulfilled human beings. God hasn't left us. We just feel as if He has. Actually He has never loved us more than at this time in our lives.

Once we have reached a certain point of growth, we must enter the furnace of affliction in order to make further progress. This is the only way in which our continuing transformation into Christ's image can be accomplished. It may be hard to see the love of God at a time like this because we associate love with feeling good and feeling secure. Yet this really is God's deepest love being expressed when we enter the stormy sea of trials and tribulations.

Here's what I believe God is allowing to happen. As we journey through our afflictions, the love we reveled in during our honeymoon period is purified. In the midst of our fires, God's love penetrates through all our superficialities into the deepest core of our being. As a result, God's love no longer lives only in our feelings and emotions. No, His love emerges out of our ashes as the one reality of our lives.

Through our many afflictions we learn that His love does not depend on our feelings, faith, or efforts. From this point on, love is much more than a feeling. It becomes the guiding principle and foundational truth for all we do. You may even be surprised to find yourself thanking God for the experience you have gone through, exclaiming with confidence the words of the psalmist,

> Where can I go from Thy Spirit?
> Or where can I flee from Thy presence?
> If I ascend to heaven, Thou art there;
> If I make my bed in Sheol, behold, Thou art there.
>
> Psalm 139:7–8

As a result of our tribulations we will now know we are loved all of the time and not just when we feel it. God's love will have become an incontrovertible fact. We will understand, no matter what happens to us and no matter how deep or how long the darkness, we will not be moved, because we are loved. Through our experiences we will have come to know, firsthand, that God will never leave us nor forsake us. I believe this is what Jesus had in mind when He said, "These things I have spoken to you, that in Me you may have peace. In the world you have tribulation, but take courage; I have overcome the world" (John 16:33).

Our honeymoon is beautiful, but there is a deeper, eternal beauty to be found in our trials. The paradox is, when we think we are dying or have been betrayed by God, we are actually on the brink of discovering the love of God like we've never seen before.

If we will truly be changed by love, we must realize God loves us for *us*. He doesn't love us for our talents. He doesn't love us for our works or efforts. He loves us for us. As a matter of fact, we just might learn that our efforts have only gotten in the way of His love.

Here's another brief poem someone sent me that I feel illustrates this point.

Broken Dreams

As children bring their broken toys
With tears for us to mend,
I brought my broken dreams to God
Because He was my friend.

But then, instead of leaving Him
In peace to work alone,
I hung around and tried to help
With ways that were my own.

At last I snatched them back and cried,
"How can you be so slow?"
"My child," He said, "What can I do?
You never did let go."

                              Author unknown

Instead of doubting God's love when everything around you is falling apart, I encourage you to seize the opportunity to reaffirm your own childlike faith in His love. It just may be that when you finally "let go," you will discover yourself being uplifted and protected like never before by your wonderfully committed "Abba" Father.

13

Giving Thanks for the Thorns

If my heart could do my thinking
And my head begin to feel
I would look upon the world anew
And know what's truly real.
Van Morrison

What time was it? I rolled over in bed, squinted my eyes so I could see the clock, and found out it was only twenty minutes after three in the morning. I didn't know why, but for some reason I was wide awake.

As I lay in bed, a stream of memories began coming back to me, memories of different trials I had been through. Even though these were all tribulations of the past that I had received healing from and had moved beyond, this morning I became aware of the wounds within me from these

trials. This troubled me. Why were these memories flood-
ing my consciousness all at the same time? Wasn't I healed?
Hadn't I seen God's hand working all these things together
for good? Perhaps I wasn't as healed as I thought I was.

As I prayed and reflected on these memories, I saw a
vision, or a picture, in my mind. I intuitively knew I was
seeing my spirit. In this vision my spirit appeared as if it
were an organ of my body. It was a roundish, almost oval-
shaped object, and all manner of wounds were gouged in
it. I knew that each wound represented a particular tribulation I had gone through. As I watched this picture, I
began feeling the pain from these wounds. They were sensitive to touch, and some looked more like open sores. Even
though in real life these tribulations were in the past (thank
God), within my vision I could see that these wounds had
produced a profound effect on my spirit.

God has brought me through all my trials. My eyes are
fixed on Him, not on my past. He has lovingly worked all
things together for good, and I'm grateful. He has created
life out of lifeless situations. His mercy has never shined
brighter than during my own dark nights in the valley of
the shadow of death. His never-ceasing faithfulness has
produced the faith I now walk in. Because of His love, I am
dedicated to seeing the good He creates out of all the things
that have touched my life, regardless of their origin.

But for some reason, early that morning, my eyes were
back on the trials of the past. Even though I've been walking in the Lord for over twenty years, I was that little child
again, calling out in pain to "Abba"—my Father.

As I lay in bed, reflecting on this strange vision, I began
telling the Lord just how dependent I was on Him. I was
overcome by this feeling that the wounds of my past had
left me in a weakened state, even though I knew God had
brought some growth through them. That spiritual "swag-
ger" and "know-it-all" attitude of my early days as a
believer were long gone. Instead of blithely thinking, "I

can do all things," I now feel that I can't do anything, not on my own. But I am glad to know my wonderful God Who can do all things.

Toward the end of this early morning meditation, God began ministering to my spirit, explaining the vision I was seeing. He impressed on me that my wounds were necessary. It was good for me to remember them and feel their pain because they kept me near Him in humility, dependence, thankfulness, and compassion. In His gentle whisper, God was telling me that the memory of my wounds brought me consciously nearer to my own Wounded Healer, Jesus Christ.

The apostle Paul wrote, "When I am weak, then I am strong" (2 Cor. 12:10). Yes, that's what the Bible says. However, if your experience has been anything like mine, you were probably taught just the opposite. You were probably taught that weaknesses are bad, not a revelation of strength in the Lord. They are to be confessed and overcome and are not pleasing to God. We should all be strong Christians, never sinning, always praising, rebuking the devil at every turn, and walking on top of all our problems.

In my early Christian years, I was continuously told that my strength was not mine but the Lord's. But I always got lost somewhere between my willpower and His power in me. Folks would tell me I couldn't do it on my own and that only God could. No sooner would that statement be out of their mouths than they'd be insisting that I make a full commitment as a completely yielded and submitted disciple to total sinless perfection and obedience to His written word. In other words, I would prove to God that I believed Him to be my strength by doing it all myself. Sound familiar? All of this spiritual double-talk left me wondering just whose strength was required to live this Christian life.

I set out determined to be God's number-one disciple. I was like Peter—"all may deny you, but not me." I think perhaps all of us start out this way in our Christian walk. And we continue walking that way until life throws a big brick wall up in front of us. However, in my own times of defeat and ignorance and, yes, even in my own sins, I have discovered strength in my weakness. It wasn't until my own willpower was completely exhausted that I was able to truly touch this reality. When all my prayers and faith didn't amount to a hill of beans, when my obedience and self-denial had completely played themselves out until there was nothing left except for me to throw in the towel, that's when I found a strength I had been unaware of up to that point. This strength wasn't just a matter of giving it one more shot. No, this new strength and faith were something that seemingly came out of nowhere. I now understand I couldn't have had this inner awareness of strength until my own efforts at trying to be the perfect Christian were out of the way.

When you give up and say you don't believe anymore and find yourself still believing anyway, even though everything in you rebels at the thought of trying once more, then you know your belief must be of the Lord. I think God allowed my Christianity to exhaust itself so I could finally get out of the way. Then, at last, He could begin living His life through me, showing me His strength, mercy, love, and wisdom. I had always confessed that "it was no longer I, but Christ" but, as I have already mentioned, I also felt pressure to rely on my own obedience, my own faith, even my own submission. So how could I possibly have been growing in the knowledge of Him when my total attention was on what I had to do?

However, my new awareness of His life within me produced a simple trust in God and His power. This was not another new commitment on my part. Well, in a sense, maybe it was. I now committed myself to stop trying on my own. From now on, if God wanted the job done, He was going to have to do it.

My faith was no longer in what I believed God would do. I wasn't looking to His actions on my behalf. No, that faith had truly died. This curious new faith that now lived within me was a faith more in who God is rather than what God does. I was now seeing "my friend who sticks closer than a brother" (Prov. 18:24). As a result of my own trials and failures, I believe God lifted me up to a higher level where I was now seeing His true nature and not merely His actions.

As I lay in bed early that morning, meditating on my vision of the wounded spirit, my thoughts turned to something Paul wrote in 2 Corinthians about his own experience. Paul declared, "I am well content with weaknesses, with insults, with distresses, with persecutions, with difficulties, for Christ's sake; for when I am weak, then I am strong" (12:10). Paul even went so far as to say, "Most gladly, therefore, I will rather boast about my weaknesses, that the power of Christ may dwell in me" (12:9). What had happened to Paul that he was able to make such a declaration? What was he seeing that enabled him to apparently *welcome* weakness? How did Paul get to the point of seeing his weakness as a blessing rather than a curse?

This declaration of joy in the midst of weakness was preceded by Paul's discussion of a thorn he had received in his flesh. This wasn't a literal splinter. The phrase, "thorn in the flesh," represented a personal problem, adversity, sin, or illness Paul was experiencing in his own life.

I've heard a lot of people speculate about Paul's thorn. Some believe it was a problem he had with his eyesight. Others have wondered if Paul was referring to a struggle with living the celibate life. Still others wonder if it might have been painful memories of the Christians he had put to death prior to his own conversion. Maybe it was none of these things. Then again maybe it was all of these things. Perhaps it was even all of these things plus other matters Paul couldn't even bring himself to write about.

Personally, I don't think we need to know what Paul's thorn was, and I'm actually glad we don't know. If we knew, for instance, that Paul was referring to his failing eyesight, I'm sure we would miss the point of the revelation he received and would probably mentally categorize this section of Scripture as being relevant only for people with eye problems. We would, therefore, miss the greater truth of the thorn in the flesh. I'm content to know simply that Paul's thorn was, in some sense, an "I" problem. With this understanding I can relate my own thorn (or thorns!) to Paul.

The thorn was not the issue. The real issue, as I see it, was Paul's perspective, or point of view, concerning his thorn. You see, as far as we know, the thorn never left Paul. At first he wanted to get rid of it, and then, after God spoke to him, Paul decided he was thankful for the thorn. What happened to Paul's understanding that caused such a radical change of mind about his thorn?

Let's also keep in mind that this whole thorn problem existed right in the midst of Paul's active ministry, while he was being mightily used of God to bring the gospel to the Gentiles. It was during this period of healing miracles, raising the dead, and planting churches throughout Greece and Asia Minor that Paul was beset by this thorn. Paul was being used of God powerfully in perhaps the single greatest ministry in existence at the time. So one insight we can gain right away is that the presence of a thorn in the flesh has nothing to do with being disobedient or out of the will of God. Paul was smack-dab in the middle of God's will when his thorn pierced him. Here, in his own words, was where Paul was, spiritually speaking, when he became aware of the thorn in his flesh. He said, "Because of the surpassing greatness of the revelations, for this reason . . . there was given me a thorn in the flesh, a messenger of Satan to buffet me—to keep me from exalting myself" (12:7).

How about that?

According to Paul (and he should know), this thorn was given to him, not as a punishment for some sin, but as a result of his great revelations! Not only that, but Paul also said this thorn was nothing less than a "messenger of Satan," sent to buffet him or beat him up.

It seems to me that Paul gained a greater understanding of himself through this thorn experience. That's part of the hidden blessing in having a thorn. He recognized that without this thorn he might have taken off on some religious ego trip. ("Look at me. I had great revelations. I'm something special. I had my revelations because I'm holier than you are.") Yes, I think Paul realized this was where he might have wound up, except for that thorn.

Of course Paul gained this insight into himself after the fact. When he first became aware of the thorn in his flesh, Paul did what any good Bible-believing Christian would do—he trusted God to remove the thorn. Any messenger of Satan needs to be rebuked, right? If this thorn were of the devil, then God's will must obviously be to cast out the thorn and claim victory over it.

He wrote, "Concerning this I entreated the Lord three times that it might depart from me" (12:8). I'm sure some believers, who still can't accept the presence of thorns in their lives (and certainly wouldn't believe that God brings good to us out of them), would say that if Paul truly believed God he should have prayed only once. Or they would say Paul gave up too soon—he should have kept on praying. Yes, some people will say anything in order to ignore the lesson of the thorn.

Paul's faith was fine. The condition of Paul's faith had nothing to do with the thorn remaining in his life. I believe the reason Paul opened his heart to share this experience with the Corinthians was so that they (and we) might benefit from the revelation he received as a result of attempting to "pray away" his thorn. Actually, if we see anything

about Paul's faith, it would be that this thorn was given to
him because he had great faith.

So Paul assumed the thorn must go. He may have rea-
soned in his heart that any hindrance to his faith must be
gotten rid of. Perhaps he thought the testimony in all this
would be, "I received a thorn, a messenger of Satan, so I
prayed, trusted God, claimed my victory, and it went
away." Maybe Paul thought this type of testimony would
strengthen the brethren. But there was just one problem—
the thorn wouldn't go away.

Paul was stuck with his thorn. He had tried prayer, and
prayer had failed to remove it. I imagine that at this point
Paul must have been in confusion. His thorn was not the
result of sin or disobedience, so I'm sure Paul must have
been trying to figure out why this was happening in his life.

But then he heard God's life-changing reply, "My grace
is sufficient for you, for power is perfected in weakness"
(12:9). God was saying, "Stop looking at the thorn and start
looking at me. Let the presence of the thorn bring you to a
complete dependence on my grace. The thorn has made
you aware of your own weakness, but my grace will make
you aware of my power. It is this blessed thorn that has
brought you this revelation."

Paul's victory was not in conquering the thorn. His great
victory was found in the humble acceptance of his thorn.
Rather than continue in the rebuking mode, viewing it as
an enemy, Paul embraced his thorn and found it to be his
friend. It wasn't until he saw God's grace being revealed
to him through his thorn, that he was able to change his
perspective or point of view concerning this thorn. Paul's
inability to remove the thorn had put him in touch with
his own weakness, and that was good. Instead of becoming haughty, which might have happened if his thorn was
removed, Paul was humbled and admitted his weakness.
It was then that God manifested His grace.

Each of us needs to know that God is with us 100 percent, with or without thorns in our lives. If we do discover

a thorn, it's good to know that God is not horrified by it. God looks at the presence of thorns in our lives as divine opportunities to reveal the incredible depth of His love and commitment to us. The issue is never "Do I have any thorns?" The issue is always "Is God a gracious God?"

I'm sure, if God had chosen to remove Paul's thorn after prayer, this testimony would have encouraged a few folks. But I believe the revelation that Paul received through the ongoing struggle is a testimony that can minister life to everyone.

How about you? Are you willing to adopt a new point of view concerning your own weaknesses? Are you willing to believe your shortcomings are nothing more than opportunities to receive a revelation of God's grace? Perhaps you've been rebuking your faults and hating yourself for having flaws. Why not give all that up and instead let God whisper the word of grace in your ear?

God's grace enables us to take the spotlight off ourselves and put it right on Him. That's why He looks particularly wonderful when He reveals His grace to us in our weakness. I believe that if you are willing to accept His grace right now, every one of your apparent weaknesses will be transformed before your eyes from being your enemy to being your friend. If you will allow your own thorns to bring you to a place of dependence on His grace, then you too will begin shouting with Paul, "Most gladly, therefore, I will rather boast about my weaknesses, that the power of Christ may dwell in me" (12:9).

Perhaps it has been the grace of God that has allowed thorns in your life, so that you may come to this point of inner freedom where, at long last, your eyes are taken off your flaws and are instead put on His great love for you, which is revealed precisely in these "flaws." The bottom line is this: Your flaws, in the hands of God, are your greatest blessings, because you can see Him in them. Rather than judging you for having flaws, God accepts your thorns (He may even create them!) and uses them as a vehicle to express His love to you. If you begin seeing this truth, you will cease being ashamed of your weaknesses and will instead be grateful to God that He continuously offers grace to you, weaknesses and all.

Instead of cursing yourself for having weaknesses, I encourage you to begin thanking God for them. Be willing to hear His voice say, "My grace is sufficient for you, for power is perfected in weakness."

This was what God was whispering in my heart that morning as I viewed the pain of my past. I had been looking at my mistakes, trials, and tribulations, and was painfully aware of my weakness. But the pain melted into relief, then into gratitude and joy, as God showed me that my wounds were good, even holy, because they kept me close to Him, dependent on Him, and near His heart.

14

$\mathcal{P}$arable of the $\mathcal{S}$hipwreck

$\mathcal{H}$e was wasting away in prison.

It had been nearly two years since Paul had been arrested in Jerusalem on trumped-up charges of defiling the temple (Acts 21–22). Invoking his right as a Roman citizen, Paul had appealed his case to Caesar. Now he and Luke (the author of Acts) were being put aboard a ship ready to set sail for Rome.

The problem was that it was late in the year, and storm season was beginning. It was a risky proposition to undertake a journey by sea right now. Some felt it would be best to winter in the harbor and wait for spring. Paul had even advised the captain of the ship to stay in port and play it safe.

However, the ship's pilot felt they should make a go for it. When a gentle south wind came up, it looked like the sign they had been waiting for, so they overrode Paul's

advice. After all, whom were they going to listen to, an old
sea dog or this prophet in chains?
They put out to sea, and at first everything was fine.

> But before very long there rushed down from the land a
> violent wind, called Euraquilo; and when the ship was
> caught in it, and could not face the wind, we gave way to
> it, and let ourselves be driven along.
>
> Acts 27:14–15

As I share this story of Paul's journey from Caesarea to
Rome, look at it as a parable for your own life, the life of
the wounded healer. Think of the ship Paul was on as rep-
resenting you. In this account we'll see a pattern concerning the stages we go through when we encounter storms
that are bigger than we are.

And isn't this what happens to us? We may be sailing
merrily along when all of a sudden a violent wind comes
out of nowhere and starts ripping our life apart. At first,
like the sailors in this story, we may try to stand up to it or
"face the wind." Yet instead of standing against the wind,
we're driven along by it.

Reading this account, I imagined a group of sailors on
the shore shouting, "Steer the ship this way! Lower the sail
that way! Do this! Do that!" It's one thing being on the
shore looking at the storm, and it's quite another thing
being out there in the middle of the storm with your ship
totally out of your control.

If you are presently going through deep, dark trials as
a Christian—trials that other believers, short of going
through their own dark night of the soul, can have no way
of understanding—people may express all kinds of well-
intentioned but completely inappropriate advice for you.
The folks who say they want to help you can, unfortunately, become the ones who are the most intolerant of you,
if they feel you won't take the simplest of steps to deliver

yourself. If someone is hitting you in the back of the head with a hammer, it's pretty hard to pay attention to anything else. That hammer commands your full attention. This, many times, is what our trials are like.

A caller on my radio program said, "I should be trusting the Lord, but the pain is so great." That's life. When you get smacked over the head, most likely you're thinking about getting smacked over the head. It's easy for someone on the sidelines to say, "Well, you ought to do this, and you ought to do that," but they're not in your shoes, and they're not relating to your pain. They may be *trying* to relate to your pain, but often the most they are able to do is relate your pain to their theology.

Not to pass judgment on anyone, but the point of the matter is, when you do go through your darkest moment, it's simply out of the realm of other people's understanding. When a Christian experiences deep trials and afflictions, other Christians often respond with fear and put up walls to protect themselves. Some may think, "If I just confess this verse, or if I just trust God, nothing like that will ever happen to me." Sometimes I think all this confession is nothing more than an expression of insecurity and a fear of the unknown, which is understandable. However, I believe it is unfair to judge someone because life has whacked that person on the side of the head—particularly if everything seems to be going well for us, and we have no point of reference for that person's pain.

> Running under the shelter of a small island called Clauda, we were scarcely able to get the ship's boat under control. And after they had hoisted it up, they used supporting cables in undergirding the ship; and fearing that they might run aground on the shallows of Syrtis, they let down the sea anchor, and so let themselves be driven along.
>
> verses 16–17

This is our natural response to the storms of life. First we try to strengthen our ship. We want to hold it together. The sailors were using supporting cables to hold the ship together. Whether we are dealing with the failure of a marriage, a physical affliction, financial distress, or some other trial, when tragedy strikes us out of the clear blue sky, our first response is usually to try to hold our ship together and hang tough—in the name of the Lord, of course. We say, "This thing will pass. The storm will end. I'll just strengthen my ship and everything will be okay." And sometimes, by the grace of God, the storm does pass. Sometimes—but, that didn't happen this time.

> The next day as we were being violently storm-tossed, they began to jettison the cargo.
>
> verse 18

Step one is trying to hold your ship together. Step two is, when you realize you can't hold your ship together, you start getting rid of cargo. In the spiritual sense (or in the sense of this account being a parable), this means you start getting rid of things you realize are not truly necessary to your faith in God. Perhaps you had an elaborate set of beliefs about God, and as long as there were no storms, everything seemed to work just fine. Then a storm comes into your life, you put your faith to work, and initially you may receive much strength and encouragement. But at a certain point, if that storm just continues beating on you, you may begin questioning everything you have believed. You start getting rid of cargo. This is part of the progression of being caught in a storm that is bigger than you are.

> And on the third day they threw the ship's tackle overboard with their own hands. And since neither sun nor stars appeared for many days, and no small storm was assailing us, from then on, all hope of our being saved was gradually abandoned.
>
> verses 19–20

Things were getting desperate for the crew of the ship. I don't wish this type of experience on a single living soul. It is the most painful thing one can go through—to be in a storm so dark and so long that "neither sun nor stars appeared for many days." This wasn't any small storm. And "from then on all hope of our being saved was gradually abandoned."

Have you ever reached that point? Perhaps you're in a situation now, and you don't even know where it came from. Maybe you've been able to get some insight and see how you helped it happen or how you walked into it with your eyes wide open. Or maybe your storm is something somebody did to you. Regardless of where it came from, when your trial just goes on and on and on, after a while you may feel your prayers are like BBs bouncing off a brick wall. Gradually all hope of being saved from the situation is abandoned. That's the worst place to be—when you're crying out, "My God, my God, why hast Thou forsaken me?"

Again, it's easy for someone to sit on the sidelines full of opinions. "Well, you just need to do this, or you just ought to do that." You've got to understand that if you're in a storm and your ship is completely beyond control and your brothers and sisters are giving you their "do this, do that" routine, they're trying their best, but they have no point of reference other than their opinions for what you're going through. They see things in light of their own experience. If they haven't lived through their own storm, their advice may miss the mark by a mile, even though they may think they're right on the money.

> And when they had gone a long time without food, then Paul stood up in their midst and said, "Men, you ought to have followed my advice and not to have set sail from Crete, and incurred this damage and loss."
>
> verse 21

This is another tortuous valley we pass through in our trials. You may say, "Oh, if only I had paid attention," or "If only I had listened to the Lord," or "If only I hadn't followed my own impulses." In this terrible place, not only do you give up all hope of being saved, but you also painfully realize your own responsibility in helping to create the very storm that is tearing you apart. You see now that if you had acted differently you might have avoided this storm altogether. This is indeed the lowest point. Hope of being saved is gone. You plague yourself with guilt and condemnation. "Oh, I wish I could back up and change it now." But you can't, because it's gone.

Okay, so you didn't follow or listen to the Lord. Is that it? Is the show over? Was this your one chance?

> And yet now I urge you to keep up your courage, for there shall be no loss of life among you, but only of the ship.
>
> verse 22

It is important to see the part we play in bringing our storms to pass. It's good to gain wisdom about ourselves so that we may avoid making the same mistake twice. But when you have seen that, then it's time to move on. That's exactly what Paul did. Just when the crew had completely given up and were up to their necks in guilt and blame, Paul began to encourage them and promise that things were going to get better.

Remember, the ship is you. It represents your safety structure. It's what you believe about life. It's your security system. If you go through a "Euraquilo" in your life, your ship may be wrecked, but you will be all right. In other words, the experience may "kill" you, but it will also reveal a new you. I guarantee that. And guess what? The new you won't be based on theory, or opinion, or believing something because so-and-so told you. From now on your new awareness of life, forged out of the fires of adversity, will be based on what really works. You're going to be okay, but your way of looking at things is going to be changed. You're going to come through this with the Lord, but you're going to have a different concept of God than you had before. This is the difference between theory and reality. Seeing this difference is a great gift from the Lord.

> For this very night an angel of the God to whom I belong and whom I serve stood before me.
>
> verse 23

It's vital for us to realize, especially in a time like this, that we belong to God. Your whole life may be falling apart. You may feel as if God has gone away on vacation and isn't one bit interested in listening to you. You may go through the various stages of initially having great faith, then a wavering faith, then no faith at all; and then, almost as a total surprise, you have faith again. But this faith is different. It's not a faith in a promise, a confession, or in a situation changing, but a simple and ultimate faith in God Himself. Sometimes it's not until you're at the end of your rope that you finally conclude, "I know whom I have believed." Or, as Job said, "Though He slay me, I will hope in Him" (Job 13:15). The severity of the storm makes you jettison all your cargo until you feel as if there's nothing left. Many times it's at that point of absolute despair that a breakthrough occurs in your heart to finally see God. Getting rid of your cargo, as painful as it is, actually clears the air for you to see God all by Himself.

> But when the fourteenth night had come, as we were being driven about in the Adriatic Sea, about midnight the sailors began to surmise that they were approaching some land. And they took soundings, and found it to be twenty fathoms; and a little further on they took another sounding and found it to be fifteen fathoms. And fearing that we might run aground somewhere on the rocks, they cast four

anchors from the stern and wished for daybreak. And as
the sailors were trying to escape from the ship, and had let
down the ship's boat into the sea, on the pretense of intend-
ing to lay out anchors from the bow, Paul said to the cen-
turion and to the soldiers, "Unless these men remain in the
ship, you yourselves cannot be saved." Then the soldiers
cut away the ropes of the ship's boat, and let it fall away.

verses 27–32

Often this is exactly what we do. We try to escape from
our situation, and usually we only make it worse. Or perhaps we are completely beaten down and can only "wish
for daybreak." But for Paul and the crew of the ship, there
was no escape now. All possible avenues of flight were
cut off.

And until the day was about to dawn, Paul was encouraging them all to take some food.

verse 33

Paul was saying, "Eat food, even though you don't think
there's a reason to." This is another stage of being in the
storm. You reach the point where you say, "Well, Lord, I've
gone through my anger with you. I've gone through the
feeling of being abandoned. I've gone through the feeling
of 'This is all my own fault.' I've lightened the ship, I've
thrown out the cargo, and I've given up all hope of being
saved." But then, just when all seems lost, you realize,
"Where else can I turn?" You come to the place where, even
in spite of everything, you still hope in the Lord. You know,
more than ever before, that God is your (only) light and
life. So you keep eating, spiritually speaking. Even though
circumstances may be saying, "You're finished," intuitively
you know you will survive.

The sailors didn't think they were going to live, so they
weren't even bothering to eat. They didn't have the
strength in them to take a bite of food. So just as the angel

told Elijah, Paul told the shipwrecked sailors, "Keep eating. Keep strengthening yourselves."

> "Today is the fourteenth day that you have been constantly
> watching and going without eating, having taken nothing.
> Therefore, I encourage you. . . ."
>
> verse 33–34

Paul took on the ministry of encouragement. To remain stuck in the "you should have listened to me" mode would have been nothing but pointless pain for the crew of the ship. That's right, they hadn't listened to Paul. But Paul let that truth go in order to bring out the greater truth, which he began to do as he encouraged the sailors.

> "Therefore I encourage you to take some food, for this is
> for your preservation; for not a hair from the head of any
> of you shall perish." And having said this, he took bread
> and gave thanks to God in the presence of all; and he broke
> it and began to eat. And all of them were encouraged, and
> they themselves also took food. And all of us in the ship
> were two hundred and seventy-six persons.
>
> verses 34–37

The crew listened to Paul, took food, and were encouraged. You see, a lot of times in the storms of life we just don't have any answers. We can get completely buried with guilt trying to find an answer, but many times there simply is no discernible rhyme or reason for what we are going through. In that situation we need to keep eating, spiritually, and allow the trial to become a revelation of God to us.

> And thus it happened that they all were brought safely to
> land.
>
> verse 44

What's the moral of this story? Paul had heard from God at the start of this account, but nobody would listen to him.

Perhaps you're thinking, why did this have to happen to Paul? Didn't he have enough troubles? Yes, he did, but because of this additional trial in Paul's life, 276 people realized that God was looking out for them.

Paul went through the storm, but it wasn't for him. It was for a total of 276 people. If there's a point to see in all of this (and this is my utter conviction), it's that when we go through times of darkness in our own lives, we reach a point where it doesn't matter where the storm came from. That's not the issue. The issue is where it's going and what it's accomplishing in our lives.

Here's what I've seen in my own life and in the lives of thousands I've counseled concerning these dark nights of the soul. Christ was wounded for our transgressions. He was broken so we might be made whole. And that's what God allows us to experience in our darkest trials. If we will humbly allow our suffering to go into the hands of God, other people will receive life through it. And this is what gives life back to us, as we see our brokenness making other people whole. We can at last see a redeeming value in our pain, because through our shipwreck, other people are being blessed. I believe this is what Paul referred to when he talked about sharing in "the fellowship of His sufferings" (Phil. 3:10).

I know this is not an easy word. God has to quicken it to your own heart. Let's say you've been through some gut-wrenching, life-breaking, completely humiliating trial; and then you come across the path of someone else who's going through a dark night of the soul. What do you feel for that person now that you have experienced your own shipwreck? If you hadn't been through it yourself, guess what you would be saying? "Just hang in there. Maybe you ought to do this. Perhaps you ought to try that." But when you've been through it yourself, you are no longer quick to criticize or to render your own opinions. Most likely your heart will be moved with compassion and you'll begin, like Paul, giving out encouragement. You'll want to bless someone; you might not have done this before. And sometimes you'll even spare people from much pain as they learn from your experience.

In the final analysis, I believe it's a rare privilege to be identified with the sufferings of Christ. If you haven't gone through your own "Euraquilo," you'll probably think there's no privilege, glory, or testimony in this whatsoever. But once you've walked through the "valley of the shadow of death" and God has brought you out to the other side (and if He hasn't yet—He will), you will be forever changed. Believe it or not, you will even find yourself one day thanking God for the experience that was the death of you, for the whole new perspective and appreciation of life that it has given you.

It's a transcendently beautiful moment when you can honestly say, from the depths of your being, "God, thank you for making me a wounded healer."

15

The Things
That Held You Down
Are Going to Carry You Up

When my son Jesse was small, I rented the movie *Dumbo, The Flying Elephant*. You know, one of the great things about having children is that you can act like a kid again and justify it by saying you are doing it for your kids. So I must confess some selfish motivation in renting *Dumbo*. I love the vintage animation of those old Disney films. Well, I often say God can speak to you anytime, anywhere, through anything He chooses. And that day, as I watched *Dumbo* with my son, the Lord chose to speak to my heart through the story of this cartoon elephant.

For those of you who are unfamiliar with the movie, Dumbo was a young circus elephant who had been born with unusually enormous ears. Because he was different, he was regarded as a freak by all the other elephants. Except for Dumbo's loving and protective mother, all the elephants ridiculed him.

Poor Dumbo. He could hardly walk without tripping over his ears, and he found himself in all kinds of trouble because of them. Oh how he wished he hadn't been cursed with those big floppy ears!

However, a small circus mouse felt sorry for Dumbo's plight and befriended him. He encouraged Dumbo to ignore the criticism of others and instead see himself as someone special. But things just seemed to go from bad to worse for Dumbo.

One particular scene in the movie marked a turning point for Dumbo. He awoke one morning to find himself and his little companion nestled in the branches of a tree. They couldn't figure out how they had gotten up there because they knew elephants couldn't climb trees. After much discussion and head scratching, they came to the conclusion that Dumbo must have somehow flown up into the branches of the tree.

At this moment of revelation the circus mouse exclaimed, "Dumbo, you can fly!" But it was the next statement from this little cartoon rodent that ministered to my heart. He looked at his perplexed elephant friend and said, "The very things that held you down are going to carry you up and up and up."

While watching this movie, I was seeing a parable. I saw a story about an individual weighed down with a personal handicap. He was different from others and was stigmatized because of this difference. Everyone made fun of him and treated him as a freak, so he grew to hate his deformity. However, when he chose to change his perspective concerning his problem, his handicap turned out to be his best friend. His deformity didn't change—*he* changed. Instead of seeing his difference as a curse, he began seeing it as a blessing. And, of course, the movie ends with

Dumbo as the big star of the circus, the famous flying elephant. So the mouse's prophetic statement proved to be true for Dumbo.

I believe we should apply the wisdom of the circus mouse to our own lives. "The very things that held you down are going to carry you up and up and up." Let God whisper this in your ear. Let Him repeat it to your heart. Keep listening until it becomes your own truth and conviction about life. "The very things that held you down are going to carry you up and up and up."

I've counseled with hundreds of people over the past seventeen years who have been in the midst of tremendously difficult and overwhelming circumstances. They've trusted God for things to get better, and they've done whatever they could to make things better, but for many of these people circumstances only seemed to go from bad to worse. However, I've seen some dramatic turnarounds, inwardly speaking, when people begin to believe that "The things that held you down are going to carry you up." When people stop being angry with God for their circumstances and stop looking for someone to blame for their situation, they are then able to begin seeing what God can make out of their situation. Adverse circumstances and handicaps are transformed into unique blessings right before our eyes when we stop looking at our situations as curses and instead start seeing God's committed hand leading us upward in Him. What was formerly a liability becomes a precious asset when we are willing to accept God's hand of anointing on it.

For instance, in counseling people who have been in a backslidden state for years, I've found that their experiences while apart from the Lord become objects of His wisdom and ministry in their lives when they are submitted to Him. I believe God sees the redeemable in everything and wishes for us to see the same. Nothing is wasted with God. Even times of rebellion and disobedience, when given to Him, become vehicles for the Holy Spirit to bring out His truth and fruitfulness in our lives.

When Peter denied knowing Christ, you could say this was a sin. But Jesus chose to look at it as a part of Peter's growth. Jesus said, "And when you have returned, strengthen your brethren" (Luke 22:32). Jesus chose not to look at the sin, but at what He could make out of that sin. In this case, Peter's failure was used by God as an instrument of humility in his life, and this helped him to strengthen his brethren more effectively. The thing that dragged him down became, in God's hands, the thing that lifted him up.

Before he came to Christ, Paul was the most zealous enemy of the church. He wanted nothing more than to stamp out this new "Jesus movement." He arrested many Christians, had them thrown into jail, and was personally responsible for the deaths of numerous believers. While this was sin of the deepest kind, when Paul submitted his life to Christ, I believe God used *all* of his past experiences to make him the minister he became. Why do you suppose Paul was so completely dedicated to the grace of God? Why was he so committed to ministering God's free salvation to all people? Don't you think God's complete forgiveness of Paul, in light of what he had done, had an even greater impact on him than if he had always been a mild, quiet-tempered person?

Perhaps you're looking at a situation in your life that is weighing you down. All you can see is your limiting circumstances. You can't even begin to imagine you would ever be grateful for this problem. But I want to tell you, in the same way the Bible says, "All things work together for good" (Rom. 8:28), your problem has a precious treasure hidden within it. When you give your liability, sin, handicap, or trial to the Spirit of God, He transforms the thing that held you down into a vehicle that will carry you up in Him.

The hard part is believing. God is ready to take your limitations, no matter what they are or where they've come from, and show you how they can be used by Him to bring you into glorious new experiences you wouldn't have dreamed possible. This is the challenge for you—to believe there are no liabilities, but only special circumstances that God desires to work for a unique good in your life.

When we're in limiting circumstances, it's easy to fall back into the self-pitying practice of making scapegoats. Rather than see how our difficulties can be turned into blessings, we shut that light off completely when we look for someone or something to blame our problem on. We may settle into an apathetic type of acceptance of our situation, saying, "My life would be better if I didn't have this problem," or "I'd be able to do more for the Lord if I wasn't bound up by this situation." Or perhaps we may develop a bitter attitude about life in general, sitting on the sidelines thinking that everyone else is blessed while we are defective.

Let's assume for a moment that all this is true. Maybe you could do more and maybe your life would be different if you didn't have your disability or limiting circumstances. But at a certain point, if you want to live, you have to be willing to get beyond this stage. Instead of looking at what you can't do, I encourage you to accept your situation, give it to God, and watch what He can make out of it. You may indeed discover God opening up a door for you that you would never have seen, except for the very limitation you have despised.

A negative, defeatist attitude only further weighs you down. Your problem isn't weighing you down. It's the way you *look* at your problem that weighs you down. The sooner you come to the place where you can honestly say, "My problem isn't weighing me down, it's my attitude that's holding me down," the sooner you will start to see those big ears becoming wings instead of weights.

For instance, if you're bound to a wheelchair, have some physical handicap or financial problem, or have fallen into some sin, instead of saying, "This thing is holding me down," I encourage you to realize it's your attitude, or point of view, that truly weighs you down, even more than the circumstance itself. I believe God is waiting for the chance to take whatever circumstance you're in and show you how this thing that held you down can carry you up and up and up. God wants to transform your apparent liability into an asset that will be uniquely yours. In God's hands this thing will become an important and integral part of your growth in Him.

One of my most vibrant examples of this principle comes from within my own family.

I hadn't seen my cousin Chuck since we were children many years ago. When a big Monbleau family reunion was organized on Cape Cod in 1987, we got a chance to be together once again. We all had a wonderful time together at our reunion, and a number of us, myself and Chuck included, went out that night to hear some music. As soon as we arrived, Chuck got out on the dance floor. In his twenties with striking good looks, Chuck was an outgoing, fun-loving, full-of-life type of guy.

Two weeks after our reunion, I received word of a terrible accident. Chuck had been at a lake with some friends and had broken his neck diving into shallow water. He lost all movement from the neck down, and for the first few weeks needed to be on a respirator in order to breathe. He also wasn't able to speak at first, which was even more painful than the paralysis, he said later.

As if that weren't enough, just a couple of months later Chuck's father (my uncle David) was suddenly diagnosed with inoperable cancer. Chuck's dad went into the hospital and quickly slipped into a coma. He remained in this state for a few days until one day, with wife and daughters at his side, David came out of his coma just long enough to say, "Straight ahead." Those were his last words. Chuck's dad slipped back into a coma and died shortly thereafter.

Chuck told me he personalized his father's last words. He said, "Ever since my accident I have lived according to the principle my father gave me, 'Straight ahead.'"

And that's exactly what my cousin has done with his life. He has gone straight ahead. He immediately entered a physical therapy program, which he presently continues. He has gained some limited movement in his left and right arms, and he continues to possess an optimistic attitude about his therapy.

But that's not all. Chuck enrolled in college and is specializing in computer programming. A paper he wrote (using a painstakingly slow process with his computer), in which he expressed his desire to work on developing computer technology to aid handicapped and physically challenged persons, won one of ten awards in a California statewide competition sponsored by IBM. His prize was a $9,000 computer system, a $10,000 voice recognition system, and $1,000 in software. The L. A. *Times* ran a feature article about Chuck's accomplishments.

But that's not all. Chuck has gotten himself a specially-equipped van and has every intention of reaching the point where he will be able to drive himself around. When I speak with my cousin now, I hear the same outgoing person who was always full of life, but now even more so. Many people who have met Chuck are amazed and uplifted by his "straight ahead" approach to life. He tells me, "Once in a while I get down about my circumstances, but I don't let it last long." It's been a few years since that fateful accident, and I can tell you that Chuck is still confidently moving "straight ahead." He joked with me once over the phone, telling me that when he wants to meet a girl at school, he wheels up next to her and says, "Mind if I sit down?"

My cousin Chuck is a tremendous, living example of what can happen when someone is willing to move straight ahead, letting the thing that held him down become the thing that carries him up and up and up. I've also seen how my cousin has become a great encouragement to others who are dealing with their own disabilities—physically, emotionally, and otherwise.

This reminds me of a meditation I once came across that I'd like to share with you. It's a brief tract called "This Thing Is from Me." The title comes from the Old Testament, from a verse in 1 Kings 12. The basic truth this tract expresses is this: If we will accept, rather than reject or deny our circumstances, then God is able to bring out precious truths that will immeasurably bless our lives.

This Thing Is from Me

My child, I have a message for you today; let me whisper it in your ear, that it may gild with glory any storm clouds which may arise, and smooth the rough places upon which you may have to tread. It is short, only five words, but let them sink into your innermost soul; use them as a pillow upon which to rest your weary head: "This thing is from Me."

Have you ever thought of it, that all that concerns you concerns Me too? "For whoever touches you touches the apple of Mine eye" (Zechariah 2:8). And "You are very precious in My sight" (Isaiah 43:4).

I would have you learn when temptations assail you and the enemy comes in like a flood that "This thing is from Me," that your weakness needs My might, and your safety lies in letting Me fight for you.

Are you in difficult circumstances, surrounded by people who do not understand you? Who never consult your taste? Who put you in the background? "This thing is from Me." I am the God of circumstances. You did not come to this place by accident; it is the very place God meant for you. Have you not asked to be made humble?

See then, I have placed you in the very school where this lesson is taught. Your surroundings and companions are only working out My will.

Are you in money difficulties? Is it hard to make both ends meet? "This thing is from Me," for I am your provider and would have you draw from and depend upon Me. "My God will meet all your needs according to His glorious riches in Christ Jesus" (Phil. 4:19). I would have you prove my promises.

Are you passing through a night of sorrow? "This thing is from Me." I am the "Man of Sorrows and acquainted with grief." I have let earthly comforters fail you. Turn to Me so that you may receive everlasting consolation.

Has some friend disappointed you? One to whom you opened your heart? "This thing is from Me." I have allowed this disappointment to come that you may learn that I am your best friend. I want to be the One you confide in.

Has someone repeated things about you that are not true? "This thing is from Me." Leave them to Me and draw closer to Me. "The salvation of the righteous comes from the Lord; He is their stronghold in time of trouble" (Psalm 37:39).

Have your plans been upset? "This thing is from Me." You made your plans and then asked Me to bless them; but I would have you let Me plan for you. "For I know the plans I have for you," declares the Lord, "plans to prosper you and not to harm you, plans to give you hope and a future" (Jeremiah 29:11).

Have you longed to do some great work for Me and instead have been laid aside on a bed of pain and weakness? "This thing is from Me." I want to teach you some of My deepest lessons. "They also serve who only stand and wait." Some of my greatest workers are those shut out from active service that they may learn to wield the weapon of all prayer.

Are you suddenly called upon to occupy a difficult and responsible position? "This thing is from Me." Trust Me. "Those who wait on the Lord will renew their strength. They will soar on wings like eagles; they will run and not grow weary, they will walk and not faint" (Isaiah 40:31).

This day I place in your hands this pot of holy oil; make use of it freely, My child. Let every circumstance that would crush you, every word that pains you, every revelation of your own weakness be anointed with it. The sting will go as you learn to see Me in all things.

"I will turn the darkness into light before them and make the rough places smooth. These are the things I will do; I will not forsake them" (Isaiah 42:16).

In this beautiful pamphlet, written by Laura A. Barter Snow, we once again see that the things that held you down become, in God's hands, the very things that lift you up and up and up. When you accept His presence and purpose in your circumstances and allow Him to weave them together for your good, then everything changes. Outwardly speaking, nothing may be different. But inwardly, oh, what a difference when we lay aside bitterness and instead embrace the higher truth that our situation is nothing less than an opportunity for God to minister to us and show us "great and mighty things, which you do not know" (Jer. 33:3).

Let me give you a little background about the Bible verse that inspired "This Thing Is from Me." Solomon, that great, wise king of Israel, had just died. His hot-headed son, Rehoboam, ascended the throne in his place. The people of Israel, wanting to establish a good dialogue and relationship with the new king, sent a delegation to Rehoboam saying, "Your father made our yoke hard; now therefore lighten the hard service of your father and his heavy yoke which he put on us, and we will serve you" (1 Kings 12:4).

Rehoboam consulted with his counselors. He first listened to the elders, who said, "If you will speak kindly to the people, they will be your servants for all your life." But Rehoboam forsook the counsel of the elders and went instead to his young friends who advocated taking a tough stand with the people of Israel. They recommended telling the people, "My father loaded you with a heavy yoke, I will add to your yoke; my father disciplined you with whips, but I will discipline you with scorpions" (v. 14). And so, because Rehoboam disregarded the wise counsel of the elders and spoke harshly to the people, the kingdom became divided. Ten tribes defected from Rehoboam to become the northern kingdom of Israel under Jeroboam, while only the tribes of Judah and Benjamin remained loyal to Rehoboam.

Things took an even bleaker turn when Rehoboam decided to go to war against Jeroboam:

> Then the Word of God came to Shemaiah the man of God, saying, "Speak to Rehoboam the son of Solomon, king of Judah, and to all the house of Judah and Benjamin and the rest of the people, saying, 'Thus says the Lord, "You must not go up and fight against your relatives the sons of Israel; return every man to his house, for this thing has come from Me."'"
>
> verses 23–24

Fortunately, the people listened to the word of the Lord and returned to their homes instead of killing their fellow countrymen.

When God said, "This thing has come from Me," did He really mean it was His will that the kingdom be divided? Was it His will that Solomon's son take such an insensitive and egotistical approach to his subjects? This thing was from God? I think it would have been hard for some people to believe it would be God's will for the kingdom to be divided. And it gets even worse because after this, Jeroboam constructed false idols for the people of Israel to worship. He was afraid that if they kept on going up to Jerusalem to worship, they would return to Rehoboam. So, to sum up, Rehoboam's harsh stance split the kingdom in two and led the people straight into idolatry. And yet God says, "This thing has come from Me."

On a certain level, this statement just cannot make any sense because the thing that supposedly came from God violated a number of His own commandments in the process. But I don't think God made Rehoboam act the way he did. I don't think it was God's perfect will that the kingdom be divided and that the people be led into idol worship. I believe the meaning of God's word was this: "What has happened has happened. We can't change the past. But if you will be willing to accept this circumstance as being from Me, then we can change the future."

Perhaps you're looking at your own life and painfully viewing some circumstance that has come upon you. Maybe your marriage is going down the tubes fast, and you so desperately want to have a Christian marriage. Yet the more you try, the worse it gets. Could it be that this thing is from the Lord? Maybe you're in some financial difficulty. You might have launched out into some venture, trusting God, and it has fallen flat. Could it be that this thing is from the Lord? Maybe you are in some physically limiting situation. Could it be that this thing is from the Lord? If you will humbly receive the truth that "this thing is from Me," I believe you will soon realize that God wants the very things that held you down to carry you up and up and up.

I'm not saying this as some kind of green light for you to sow a path of destruction and then glibly say, "This thing is from the Lord." This truth is not an excuse for us to go and do our own thing. We need to remember another important principle in our lives—we reap what we sow.

However, if you do find yourself in some disabling situation, I believe there is real power in this word. Instead of developing a bitter, hard-hearted attitude against God, your spouse, a business partner, your handicap, or anything else, if you will "keep your eyes on the light" and accept this thing as being from the Lord, you will then be able to see God within you, working these circumstances together for your own personal good. Instead of being overcome with anger, you can be overcome with God's healing touch on your heart. You can say, "God is in this thing. It's me He wants to work on—not the other person." Then you will see the shackles falling off and the circumstances that held you down will begin to lift you up—up into God's redeeming love and up into a positive, affirming attitude toward life. You'll be free of the illusion of your limitations, and you'll fly upward into the realm of God's power working all things together for good for you. This, indeed, is a truth that sets you free.

Dumbo could have kept looking at his ears and said, "Ah, no. It's always been a problem, and it's always going to be a problem." If he had done that, he never would have been able to fly above his circumstances. If he had let the opinions and words of others define who he was or what he could do, he would have remained stuck forever, lamenting his disability. Do you see what I'm getting at?

You may be looking at your own problem and thinking, "It's always been a problem, and it's always going to be a problem. Nothing's ever going to change. I'm never going to be able to do what God wants me to do." If that's your belief, then most likely that will be your reality. But do you know what? If you'll stare your problem straight in the eye and say, "The thing that held me down is going to carry me up. My God is bigger than my circumstance," then everything will change because you will have changed the way you look at the situation. I encourage you to let even your most difficult circumstance, no matter how far down it has dragged you, be used by our gracious Lord to lift you up. Through your difficulties, He can anoint and empower you as a wounded healer.

You may even have left God and walked straight into some sin, knowing exactly what you were doing. Perhaps you were eagerly anticipating some pleasure, only to realize afterward just how much you really blew it. Even if this is the case, I encourage you to say, "This thing is from the Lord." It doesn't mean God made you sin. It just means there's something greater than your sin in your circumstances that God wants to produce in you for your healing and for His glory.

No matter where you've been or what you've done, and no matter what has happened to you, there is a higher level of understanding and a higher spiritual law at work. When you are willing to humbly place the totality of your life in the hands of God, accepting whatever circumstances you're in as being a gift from Him, then you'll begin to rise up on eagles' wings. Instead of being bitter, negative, scapegoating, and defeated, let God show you that in His hands, your situation uniquely qualifies you for a special mercy and ministry He will give you. You will be able to see your wounds becoming avenues of God's divine healing, blessing, and restoration in others' lives as well as your own. No matter how long you've been down, I encourage you to rise up now in the compassion of our own Wounded Healer, Jesus Christ and watch as the very things that held you down carry you up and up and up.